PEOPLE AND PRODUCTIVITY

The New York Stock Exchange Guide to Financial Incentives and the Quality of Work Life

PEOPLE AND PRODUCTIVITY

The New York Stock Exchange Guide to Financial Incentives and the Quality of Work Life

William C. Freund and Eugene Epstein

DOW JONES-IRWIN   Homewood, Illinois 60430

ISBN 0-87094-510-6

Library of Congress Catalog Card No. 84–71126

Printed in the United States of America

1 2 3 4 5 6 7 8 9   BC   1 0 9 8 7 6 5 4

To Mil Batten
*For the idea that became this book
and for his unflagging support and encouragement.*

"The most valuable of all capital is
that invested in human beings."
Alfred Marshall

Foreword

Two years ago, the business pages of *The New York Times* carried a striking article that applies directly to the subject of this book.[1] The article compared the level of productivity of two different automobile assembly plants. According to the *Times*, in the first plant it took 21 worker-hours to produce a car, while in the second it took 40—a gap in performance of almost 2 to 1. In addition, the cars from the more productive plant had a lower reject rate. Most of us might guess that the better performing plant was more automated or that it used more advanced technological processes. But in fact, both plants were owned by Ford Motor Company, both turned out the same kind of car, and both had virtually identical capital equipment. The more productive plant was located in West Germany, the less productive in England. And the only way to account for the enormous difference in performance between one plant and the other was the vital factor of *people.*

This book is a greatly expanded version of a study the New York Stock Exchange published more than a year ago under its own auspices. The additional material is a comprehensive discussion of financial incentive plans, which we call *gainsharing*. The original study was the fifth[2] in a series in which productivity—the amount a worker can produce in an hour—was the main subject. The four earlier studies emphasized the "capital side" of productivity improvement. They examined what could be done to increase the rate of investment in new

---

[1]Steve Rattner, "A Tale of Two Ford Plants," *The New York Times*, October 13, 1981, Section D, pp. 1, 4.

[2]Our previous studies are: *Reaching a Higher Standard of Living*, January 1979; *Building a Better Future*, December 1979; *Productivity and Inflation*, April 1980; and *U.S. Economic Performance in a Global Perspective*, February 1981.

plant and equipment and to improve the technology embodied in that investment. By contrast, our fifth study was the first to focus on the "people side." It asked what we could do to boost productivity by better utilizing our people. The enormous interest that study engendered caused us to seek its wider distribution in the form of this book.

Underlying all our studies has been the assumption that rising living standards matter, that a better material life for our people is an essential part of a better quality of life. And from that standpoint (to borrow a phrase from a national pastime), productivity isn't everything, it's the only thing. The simple fact is that without a rise in output per worker-hour, there can be no sustained growth in income per person.

This book includes the results of the first nationwide survey of human resource programs to boost productivity in U.S. corporations. One of the main findings of the survey is that companies are giving high marks to the set of approaches generally associated with "Quality of Work Life" (QWL). Basically Quality-of-Work-Life programs encourage employees to participate in the key decisions that affect and determine day-to-day work patterns. Earlier literature on the subject had reported a number of cases in which QWL programs had proved successful. Based on our survey, I am happy to report that these cases are not isolated, but turn out to be representative of companies generally.

As with all our studies, *People and Productivity* was prepared by NYSE's Office of Economic Research under the supervision of Dr. William C. Freund, senior vice president and chief economist; senior economist Eugene Epstein served as principal writer of the final work. It is particularly fitting that this book be dedicated to William M. Batten, the chairman under whom I served for a number of years and whom I have the privilege of succeeding in that post. Throughout his long career, he exemplified the principles of humane management that this book so eloquently espouses.

John J. Phelan, Jr., Chairman
New York Stock Exchange, Inc.

Preface

If there has been one fundamental problem ailing the U.S. economy over the past decade, then that problem is lagging growth in output per worker-hour, which we define as productivity. In the 1950s and 60s, productivity grew at an average rate of about 3 percent a year. Since 1973, the rate of growth has been no more than about 1 percent. While the causes of the problem are a matter of much debate, the possible cures are in broad terms quite simple and straightforward.

There are three main ways for people to increase their productivity. The first way is by acquiring *more capital*—say, an extra tractor or an extra computer. The second is by acquiring *better capital*—an improved tractor or computer. The third way is by *working smarter* with the capital they have. This book is about that third way: about the "human capital" side of boosting productivity in the workplace.

How important is the people factor in boosting productivity? The potential for better management of people is enormous; accordingly, the potential is also there for this factor to make unprecedented contributions to a rise in productivity. To take one instance, we cite results showing an average rise in productivity of 20 percent over a single year among more than 70 companies that had instituted a particular human resource program.[1] When we explore the implications of that performance, we come up with projections that almost defy belief. To begin with, assume that similar human resource programs were instituted in every American workplace and that the results showed the same increase of 20 percent over

---

[1] See Chapter 3, pages 36–37.

one year. That 20 percent would mean a growth in GNP of 20 percent. To gain perspective on this number, note that from 1973 to the present, GNP has grown by no more than 20 percent. In other words, from this factor alone, GNP would grow in one year at a rate that previously took nine. Even assuming that this 20 percent growth in productivity takes not one year but five would mean an annual rate of growth of almost 4 percent, or approximately the same rate as in the high-growth decade of the 1960s. And that assumes no contribution at all from the effects of more and better capital or from a growing labor force.

We begin this book by taking a comprehensive look at financial incentive plans, which we call gainsharing. Our coverage of the subject builds from the narrowest of such approaches to the broadest: all the way from individual incentive plans to group plans to profit sharing and employee ownership. Our aim is not to come out for any particular approach, but to explain clearly and impartially the advantages and disadvantages of each. If we favor anything, it is that all companies give gainsharing serious consideration as a means of boosting productivity.

We next take a close look at Japan, the country that more than any other has been held up as a model for Americans to emulate. People who read these pages should have a surprise in store for them. Our appreciation of the Japanese example begins with a candid look at some of the things that the Japanese cannot (and should not) teach Americans about people and productivity. And some of those things that we find Americans should learn from the Japanese are quite different from what the popular treatments of the subject have concluded.

The final section of this book summarizes the findings of the first broad-based survey of human resource programs to boost productivity. We wanted to find out how many corporations have programs, what kinds of programs these are, why these programs were introduced, how many employees are involved, and most important of all, what effect these programs have had on boosting productivity. The results are extremely encouraging, and they have important implications. The movement to boost productivity through human resource programs is still a minority movement; but through a better understanding of its successes, it may yet become a movement of the majority. The potential for boosting productivity growth through better management of people appears enormous.

A personnel executive we know was trying to persuade the plant managers in his company to consider adopting gainsharing approaches for their employees. He pointed out that when a company shares the financial gains of increased productivity, each side comes out a winner, since there is more to go around for all. The response he got was surprising. No one among his listeners doubted that companies using gainsharing were getting their workers to be more productive. But they questioned the competence of managers who needed to resort to such approaches. Wasn't it the first duty of a manager to get results out of his employees without, so to speak, having to bribe them? So wasn't gainsharing a crutch that no self-respecting manager needed to use?

One response our personnel executive didn't make, but might have, was to ask whether such things as salaries, benefits, raises, promotions—or even decent working conditions—were also crutches, since they too helped managers motivate their people. The whole range of activities described in this book are no different; they are additional tools, many of them with exciting potential, for making the American workplace more productive.

William C. Freund
Eugene Epstein

Acknowledgments

A number of experts provided advice and information; most of them also read parts of this manuscript and made suggestions for its improvement. These experts include Mitchell Fein, Jeff Gates, Luis Granados, John Kendrick, Norm Kurland, Mary Ann Maguire, Tom McCann, Bert Metzger, Richard T. Pascale, Tom Rohlen, Richard Sabo, Isaac Schapiro, and Robert Scott. We carefully considered all their suggestions and incorporated many of them. A lot of what is right with this manuscript can be credited to these people; all of what is wrong remains our responsibility.

We owe many debts to our fellow workers at the New York Stock Exchange. Ira Gelb gave us helpful suggestions every step of the way. Kenneth Fox provided first-rate research. NYSE librarians Jean Tobin and Ellen Duttweiler remained true to their oath to get us every piece of literature, no matter how obscure, on any subject imaginable. Edward Connors and William Case of NYSE's survey research department conducted our human resources survey. And Jessica Ransom performed a thousand indispensable chores. To all of them, thanks.

Finally, we wish to thank our wives, Linda Epstein and Judith Freund, for their support and encouragement.

E. E.

W. C. F.

Contents

Section 1   Sharing the Gains

1. **The Hierarchy of Incentives: What Gainsharing Is   3**
    The 100 Percent Bonus. Discretionary Effort. The New
    York Stock Exchange Survey. The Four Main Kinds of
    Gainsharing. Gainsharing and Discretionary Effort.

2. **Individual Incentive Plans: The Rehabilitation of an
    Old Idea   13**
    Individual Incentives and Gainsharing. Piecework and
    "Scientific Management." How It Works. The Future of
    Individual Incentives.

3. **Group Incentives I: Physical Productivity Plans   25**
    The Inverted Pyramid Again. Improshare: *Output per
    Worker-Hour. The Company's Share. Raising
    Standards. New Capital Equipment. Two Myths. Track
    Record.* Customized Plans: *Novel Measures of
    Performance. Complexity versus Simplicity.*

4. **Group Incentives II: Economic Productivity Plans   43**
    The Scanlon Plan. The Rucker Plan: *The Formula.
    Excluded Costs. The Two-Way Street. Physical
    Productivity versus Economic Productivity.* Addendum:
    Calculating the Bonus under the Rucker Plan: *Example
    1. Example 2. Example 3.*

5. **Industrial Homesteading: Profit Sharing and Employee
    Ownership   59**
    Lincoln Electric: *Nature versus Nurture. The Yearend
    Bonus. The Stock Purchase Plan. Guaranteed
    Employment. Job Security and Gainsharing. The Basic
    Approach.* Other Reasons: *ESOPs. Stock Purchase
    Plans. As a Pension Plan. Saving Jobs: Wage
    Concessions. Saving Jobs: Employee Buyouts. Fostering
    Democracy.* Taming Inflation. Conclusion.

**Section 2   *A Tale of Two Countries: What the United
           States Can Learn from Japan***

6. **The Effects of Discrimination: Some Things We
    Shouldn't Learn   85**
    A New Faith. Discrimination and Productivity. The
    Japanese College: A Four-Year Vacation.

7. **Preparing People for Work I: Schooling   91**
    The Importance of Schooling in Japan. U.S. Schools.
    The Need for Action. What Business Can Do.

8. **Preparing People for Work II: Training Managers   99**
    Front-Lines Experience. A Long Apprenticeship.
    Applicability.

9. **East Meets West: Japanese-Owned Businesses in the
    United States   105**
    Findings. Method. A Better Place to Work. Japanese
    Thoughts on American Workers. Quantity and Quality.
    Applicability to American-Owned Firms.

**Section 3   Human Resource Programs for Productivity:
Findings of an NYSE Survey**

10. The Programs   119
Survey Scope. Prevalence of Programs. Why Programs
Were Initiated. Types of Human Resource Activities.
The QWL Movement. Attitudes toward Participative
Decision Making. Some Advice to Those Considering a
Human Resource Program.

11. The Results   133
Productivity Impact of Individual Activities. General
Improvements Resulting from Programs. Overall
Assessment. The Potential.

Conclusion   139
Gainsharing: *Individual Incentives. Group Incentives.
Profit Sharing and Employee Ownership.* Learning from
the Japanese: *Schools. Training Managers. Applicability
of Japanese Management to the United States.* The
NYSE Survey. People and Productivity. The Quality of
Life: Both End and Means.

Appendix 1   149

Appendix 2   NYSE Survey Methodology   **164**

Bibliography   169

Index   175

> *"An ever-increasing number of citizens [should] have two sources of income—a paycheck and a share of the profits."*

Ronald Reagan, February 1975

Section 1

Sharing the Gains

"Permeate your company with an incentive philosophy. Shoot your organization through with incentives from bottom to top. Create, to the extent possible, a hierarchy of incentives from individuals on up—through small teams, departments, plants— to the entire corporation."

Bert Metzger, president, Profit Sharing Research Foundation

Chapter 1

The Hierarchy of Incentives: What Gainsharing Is

The 100 Percent Bonus

Richard Sabo, an employee at the manufacturing firm of Lincoln Electric, recalls the brief but memorable period when the company paid him nothing for his labor. Assigned to produce a particular part, he worked for nearly two days before he learned that all his output was defective. Of course, had he been at almost any other company, then he would have received his hourly wage anyway. But at Lincoln Electric they do things differently. Sabo was working under the company's piecework system, according to which all the dollars you get depend on the quantity of your usable output; if you produce nothing you're paid nothing. Sabo, now Lincoln Electric's manager of educational services, admits that his zero wage may have been in technical violation of the minimum wage laws. But even when it happened, he thought his treatment was perfectly fair. After all, the company hadn't made anything from the two days either, so why should it pay him for wasted work?

Lincoln's "zero base" piecework plan is just one component in its extensive system of *gainsharing*—the umbrella term we will use for tying all or part of employee pay to productivity or financial performance rather than to a fixed wage. It is Lincoln's gainsharing system plus some of the attendant policies that help make attitudes like Sabo's typical of the company's employees.

The piecerates affect about half of Lincoln's 2,600 people. In addition, Lincoln pays all employees an annual bonus, out of pretax profits, that is computed as a percent of each person's wage; over the past several years the percentage has averaged 100 percent—and that isn't a misprint. Also, Lincoln has a stock purchase plan. Any employee with more than one year of service can purchase stock in the company at book value. As a result, over 40 percent of the total stock of the company is in the hands of about 75 percent of the employees.

We will have more to say about this extraordinary company in the next few chapters—about its employment guarantee, its huge wage payouts, and the extremely high rate of productivity that helps makes both of these things possible. If there is a Mount Everest of gainsharing, then Lincoln Electric is it. But since mountains can be emulated only up to a point, we'll also be looking at some of the lesser peaks in order to learn from more "normal" experience with gainsharing plans.

Discretionary Effort

In the sense that we use the term, *gainsharing* will include any kind of financial incentive plan tied to individual, group, or company performance. If two recent nationwide surveys are to be believed—the first taken of the American worker, the second of American corporations—then gainsharing may be an idea whose time came long ago.

In a recently published report, pollster Daniel Yankelovich uses a concept that deserves a permanent place in the textbooks on economics. That concept is "discretionary effort." Yankelovich defines discretionary effort as "the difference between the maximum amount of effort and care an individual could bring to his or her job, and the minimum amount of effort required to avoid being fired or penalized."[1] He points out that the idea is similar to its better-known counterpart, "discretionary income." Discretionary income is that portion of an individual's income that is left after necessities and taxes have been paid—that portion, in other words, over which one has the greatest control. Similarly, an individual has greatest control over his or her discretionary effort.

The Yankelovich study provides fresh evidence of the link between discretionary effort and gainsharing. To begin with, the study concludes that the exercise of discretionary effort in the American workplace is distressingly low. Basing his findings on in-depth interviews of a cross section of American workers, Yankelovich reports that "nearly half of all jobholders (44 percent) say that they do not put much effort into their jobs over and above what is required to hold on to a job." He also found that "fewer than one out of four jobholders (23 percent) say that they are currently working at their full potential" and that "the overwhelming majority (75 percent) say that they could be significantly more effective on their jobs than they are now."[2]

Why the poor performance? According to Yankelovich, one important cause is "the degree to which the American

---

[1]Daniel Yankelovich and John Immerwahr, *Putting the Work Ethic to Work: A Public Agenda Report on Restoring America's Competitive Vitality* (New York: Public Agenda Foundation, 1983), p. 1. In the text we cite Yankelovich as sole author for the sake of brevity. Yankelovich and Immerwahr take the term *discretionary effort* from the work of the Harvard economist Harvey Leibenstein.

[2]Yankelovich and Immerwahr, *Putting the Work Ethic to Work*, pp. 2, 3.

workplace has undercut the link between a jobholder's pay and his or her performance":

> Our survey provides evidence that many people in the work force are deeply concerned about the lack of connection between their effort and their pay. More than 6 out of 10 working Americans (61 percent) identified "pay tied to performance" as a feature they wanted more of on their present job.[3]

In other words, it seems that the American worker is proposing gainsharing as a way to boost discretionary effort. The results of a New York Stock Exchange survey confirm the wisdom of that recommendation.

The New York Stock Exchange Survey

Does gainsharing work? Let's ask the people who've tried it.

As part of our survey of American corporations on their human resource programs to boost productivity,[4] the New York Stock Exchange asked whether these programs included gainsharing plans. We found that of the approximately 7,000 U.S. corporations with 500 employees or more, 15 percent have some kind of gainsharing plan. Although all size classifications and all types of industries are represented, these plans are somewhat more common among companies with greater numbers of employees.

Survey results also suggest that far more than most companies, companies with gainsharing plans maintain an open and participative atmosphere among their workers. For instance, we found that a high percentage of these companies maintain quality circles (which are problem-solving work groups). As Figure 1–1 shows, quality circles are in use at

---

[3]Ibid., pp. 26, 27.

[4]We discuss the results of this survey in greater detail in Section 3 of this book.

Figure 1–1
Proportion of Gainsharing Companies with Quality Circles (companies with 500 or more employees)

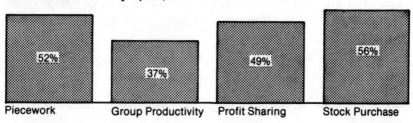

Piecework   Group Productivity   Profit Sharing   Stock Purchase

anywhere from 37 percent to 56 percent of these companies, depending on the particular gainsharing plan. These figures are far out of proportion to U.S. companies generally; according to our survey, there are quality circles at approximately 14 percent of U.S. corporations with 500 or more employees.

What is even more striking is the percentage of gainsharing companies reporting that their nonmanagement employees participate in decision making. As Figure 1–2 shows, the range is between 63 percent and 82 percent, depending on the gainsharing plan. The connection between employee decision making and gainsharing is not just coincidence. As we'll see later on, financial participation in a company often requires other forms of participation as well.

Figure 1–2
Proportion of Gainsharing Companies with Employees Involved in Decision Making (companies with 500 or more employees)

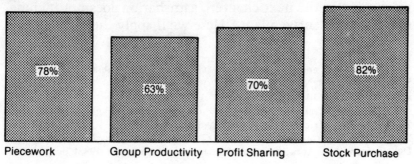

Piecework   Group Productivity   Profit Sharing   Stock Purchase

Finally, we asked these companies if their gainsharing programs were successful in terms of improving productivity. As Table 1–1 shows, positive responses ranged from more than three out of five (61 percent) to almost four out of five (77 percent).

Clearly, something's out there.

Table 1–1
Success at Improving Productivity among Gainsharing Companies (in percent)

	Piecework	Group Productivity	Profit Sharing	Stock Purchase
Successful	77%	74%	73%	61%
Unsuccessful	3	2	5	15
Too early to evaluate	0	16	2	12
Don't know	1	0	0	1
No response	19	8	20	11

The Four Main Kinds of Gainsharing

One sure sign that a term is catching on is when people start arguing over what it does and does not mean. Gainsharing is a case in point. For instance, according to an article in the *National Productivity Review*, gainsharing is *"NOT an incentive plan"* and *"NOT a worker motivation program."*[5] According to two other specialists on the subject (whose viewpoint we discuss in the next chapter), gainsharing does not include individual incentive plans.[6] Here we'll apply the term to any

---

[5]R. J. Bullock and Patti F. Bullock, "Gainsharing and Rubik's Cube: Solving System Problems," *National Productivity Review*, Autumn 1982, pp. 397, 398. Italics and caps are in the original.

[6]See Carla O'Dell, "Sharing the Productivity Payoff," *Productivity Brief*, no. 24 (Houston: American Productivity Center, undated), p. 2. Also see Robert J. Doyle, *Gainsharing and Productivity: A Guide to Planning, Implementation, and Development* (New York: American Management Association, 1983), pp. 3–4.

program in which a company shares with employees the cash rewards of improved productivity or financial performance.

In the chapters that follow, we'll often be referring back to the inverted pyramid shown in Figure 1–3.[7] Notice that we have placed on different "rungs" of the pyramid four main ways of sharing gains with workers: individual incentive plans, group incentive plans, profit sharing, and employee ownership. Each plan's position on the pyramid indicates two different things about it: first, *the horizon of financial responsibility* that the plan requires of each worker (an idea we'll be clarifying in the paragraphs that follow); and second, the *fit* it provides between individual effort and reward. We measure horizon of financial responsibility along the pyramid's width: at the widest part of the pyramid, the horizon of individual responsibility for the financial performance of the company is at its widest; at the bottom point, the horizon is at its narrowest. As we move up the pyramid then, employee responsibility for the financial performance of the company increases. But as we move down and as our arrows indicate, there is a greater focus on individual effort: At the bottom point, there is a maximum fit between individual effort and reward; at the topmost part, the fit is much looser.

Working our way up the pyramid, we begin with individual incentive plans in which a worker's income is tied partly or wholly to personal output. Under individual incentives, there is the closest fit of all between personal effort and reward; the worker gets paid according to what he or she produces. On the other hand, there is minimum responsibility for any of the other factors that help determine the financial performance of the entire company. The individual's compensation does not directly depend either on the level of company sales and profits or even on the productivity of other workers.

At Lincoln Electric, for example, about three quarters of

---

[7]This taxonomy is adapted from an idea originally outlined to a New York Stock Exchange interviewer by Bert L. Metzger, president of Profit Sharing Research Foundation, Evanston, Illinois.

Figure 1–3
Gainsharing: The Hierarchy of Incentives

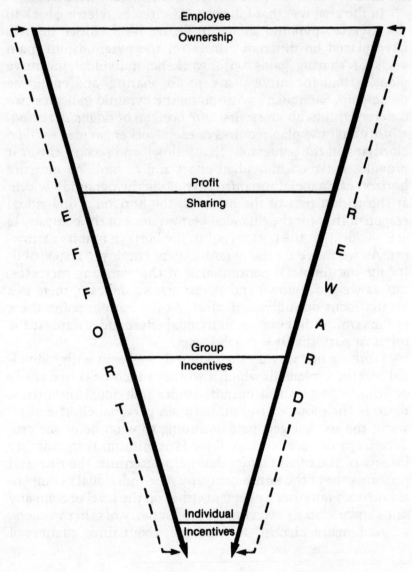

the employees on a piecerate system are working on an individual basis. And as we've mentioned, at Lincoln the entire wage for workers on piecerates is a function of how much they produce. (Also, given Lincoln Electric's formula for how profit sharing is computed, even the profit sharing will be zero on any day that their piecerate wage is zero.) At most other companies, such as The Maytag Company and Deere & Company, piecerates are part of a bonus plan that reward the individual for producing beyond a certain standard. Although piecerates conjure up an image of the sweatshop, they are compatible with any kind of work environment—and as our examples attest, they aren't necessarily a way of cheating the worker. Lincoln, Maytag, and Deere claim to pay the highest wages in their industries. Of course, salespeople and waiters and waitresses are often on individual incentive plans.

Under group incentive plans, there is a looser fit between personal effort and reward; someone may be producing a great deal but may receive no bonus if others in the group are slacking. But for the same reason, under group incentives, the worker is responsible for the synergy of group effort, not just for personal effort. Since the horizon of responsibility widens, we place group incentives next on the pyramid.

The standard group incentive plans such as Scanlon, Rucker, and Improshare, generally try to define the working group as broadly as possible. Usually this turns out to be an entire plant, with all employees covered, including salaried.

Some group incentive plans go beyond a simple measure of physical output to include other elements. For instance, the Scanlon and Rucker plans use formulas that are based in part on company sales. In addition, all the standard group incentive plans can include ways of rewarding workers not only for producing more but for making more effective use of other inputs, including materials, tools, and energy.

Profit sharing, which is next on the pyramid, broadens the worker's horizon of responsibility still further by tying the bonus to the company's bottom line. It also loosens even further the fit between individual incentive and reward. A company can be unprofitable even if its output per worker is high and even if its workers are saving on other inputs. And it can be very profitable even if its workers are doing neither of these things.

Finally, there is employee ownership, which requires full responsibility—for the output of the working group, for the marketing effectiveness of the company, and for all the factors beyond the company's control that might determine the value of its stock.

Of course, as the Lincoln Electric case attests, none of these approaches are mutually exclusive: Lincoln offers versions of them all. But whether in combination or separately, they present a series of trade-offs that are important to evaluate.

Gainsharing and Discretionary Effort

The idea of discretionary effort helps clarify the economic rationality of sharing gains with workers. Generally speaking, workers are not paid for their discretionary effort; they are paid to meet the minimum standards of performance that the company imposes. For this "acceptable effort," they are paid a competitive wage. But when workers are exercising discretionary effort, the company can pay them more than the going rate. That effort produces financial gains for the company over and above the returns it makes for acceptable effort; so the company can afford to share those gains. In other words, the company can motivate discretionary effort by practicing gainsharing.

The chapters that follow will be a guided tour of the four kinds of gainsharing we've outlined above. The main question we'll try to answer is, What trade-offs does each approach offer from the standpoint of motivating discretionary effort?

"A central theme of our cultural heritage supports the idea that individuals will fail or succeed though their own effort and hard work. When people receive equal rewards regardless of effort or achievement, the implicit message from management is: 'We don't care about extra effort, so why should you?'"

Daniel Yankelovich and John Immerwahr[1]

Chapter 2

Individual Incentive Plans: The Rehabilitation of an Old Idea

In this chapter we begin our guided tour of the four main kinds of gainsharing approaches with the stepchild of gainsharing: individual incentive plans.

Individual Incentives and Gainsharing

As we mentioned in the previous chapter, two specialists on the subject, Carla O'Dell and Robert J. Doyle, exclude individual incentives from the definition of gainsharing. Since the writings of both these people are insightful and informative

---

[1]*Putting the Work Ethic to Work: A Public Agenda Report on Restoring America's Competitive Vitality* (New York: The Public Agenda Foundation, 1983).

and since their opinion on this matter is representative of the gainsharing movement generally, their viewpoint is worth considering.

Carla O'Dell writes, "Individual incentive plans, such as piece rates or commissions, may be appropriate and effective reward systems, but they are not gainsharing. Individual incentives tend to put worker output ahead of plant or group output and lack a focus on overall productivity gains."[2]

As we explained in the previous chapter, individual incentives keep the employee's horizon of responsibility toward the company at its narrowest, which is why we placed them at the bottom point of our inverted pyramid. So O'Dell is quite right to speak of the danger that individual incentives will put worker output ahead of plant or group output; there is nothing in individual incentives that will make the worker care about group output. But to recognize that this pitfall exists should not be a reason to exclude individual incentives from the definition of gainsharing. In a well-managed company, people can be made to appreciate the obvious stake they have in a company that is successful in all its parts, not just the part that directly affects them.

Indeed, just as there are dangers from a narrow prospective, there are also dangers that arise from gainsharing plans whose prospective is broad. For instance, under a plantwide gainsharing plan, some workers may be producing a great deal but may receive a diminished bonus if others in the plant are slacking. Under those circumstances, putting plant or group output ahead of worker output can cause problems; some workers may begin to hold back if they feel that others aren't doing their share. Here again, the way to correct the problem is effective management. Managers must be ready to take appropriate action if they find that some workers are contributing far more than others.[3]

---

[2]Carla O'Dell, "Sharing the Productivity Payoff," *Productivity Brief*, no. 24 (Houston: American Productivity Center, undated), p. 2.

[3]For mention of this kind of problem arising under a plantwide incentive plan, see "A Productivity System that Works," *Boardroom Reports*, June 1, 1981.

Elsewhere in her writings, O'Dell lists the following among "minus factors" regarding individual incentive plans: they can "cause opposition to changes in methods or machinery . . . lead to a situation in which standards become contract bargaining issues . . . create difficulty in setting accurate standards [and] create peer pressure to restrict output." She goes on to write, "The employees say, 'If I produce over standard, they will change the standard on me.' "[4]

But as O'Dell herself comments, "Many of the minus factors stem from workers' distrust of management."[5] And that is just the point: Any kind of incentive plan will suffer in an atmosphere of mistrust. In particular, there is nothing inherent in group incentives that will prevent informal quotas, opposition to changes in methods or machinery, or situations in which standards become bargaining issues. Indeed, as we'll see in the next chapter, people who devise group incentive plans are painfully aware of just these very problems; a part of their job is to recommend ways of surmounting them. As O'Dell would be the first to agree, an atmosphere of trust is necessary to all incentive plans, whether individual or otherwise.

Robert J. Doyle speaks of individual incentives as belonging to a bygone era—to the "first half of this century," when "work measurement" first became popular. According to his account, group incentive plans, which he identifies with gainsharing, evolved out of widespread dissatisfaction with individual incentives; while many companies simply abandoned incentives altogether, others developed more group oriented approaches as a way to deal with the inadequacies of individual incentive plans.[6] But as Doyle readily agrees, companies often had problems with individual incentives not because there was anything inherently wrong with them, rather it was

---

[4]Carla O'Dell, *Gainsharing: Involvement, Incentives, and Productivity* (New York: American Management Association, 1981), p. 22.

[5]Ibid.

[6]Robert J. Doyle, *Gainsharing and Productivity* (New York: American Management Association, 1983), p. 3.

because the plans were poorly administered. And as Doyle also agrees, individual incentives are flourishing in plenty of companies today.[7]

What Doyle and O'Dell really seem to be talking about is a philosophical preference. According to a respectable and possibly valid managerial philosophy, all incentive plans should encourage a sense of belonging to and supporting the group. We might even say that our inverted pyramid shows different rungs on the evolutionary ladder. Doyle's historical account implies that society has evolved beyond the individual incentives rung and is now ready to step up to the group incentives rung; perhaps this too is a way station up to the highest rung of all, which is employee ownership. In other words, the broadening horizon of responsibility that group incentives afford people will help prepare them for the broadest horizon of all that comes with direct ownership.

That is an attractive viewpoint, and it is a perfectly valid basis on which to justify a definition of gainsharing. But you can also say that from the standpoint of simply motivating discretionary effort, all the rungs on the pyramid can be considered to be gainsharing, including individual incentive plans.[8]

In any case, individual incentive plans are quite compatible with the other elements that are commonly associated with gainsharing—namely, an open atmosphere in which employees are involved in decisions that directly affect their work situation. For instance, Lincoln Electric, the company with the zero-base individual incentive plan we described in

---

[7]Last two sentences in paragraph based on telephone interview with Robert Doyle, October 25, 1983.

[8]Lest it be thought that including individual incentive plans under the rubric of gainsharing is especially radical, we might cite for support no less a source than the Institute of Industrial Engineers (IIE). According to IIE's publication, *Industrial Engineering Terminology* (approved December 9, 1982), gainsharing is "a financial incentive plan in which the savings from improved productivity (savings gained) are shared between the company and the *employee*" (page 236, italics added). The use of the singular "employee" indicates that this definition can be applied to individual incentive plans.

the first chapter has what it calls an advisory board of elected employee representatives. Every two weeks, the advisory board meets with top management to discuss matters of mutual concern. In addition, Lincoln's piecework system itself permits a decentralization of authority; people on piecerates work pretty much as independent subcontractors responsible for the quantity and quality of their own output. This system is part of the reason why Lincoln is able to maintain approximately 1 supervisor for every 100 workers, compared with a manufacturing industry range of 10 to 25 workers for every supervisor. In general, there is far less need to supervise people who are paid by the piece rather than by the hour.

Piecework and "Scientific Management"

Another source of hostility to individual incentives springs from the tendency to associate them with the principles of "scientific management" supposedly developed by the famous turn-of-the-century engineer Frederick Winslow Taylor. We say supposedly only because managerial consultant Peter F. Drucker has recently argued that Taylor's theories have been "totally misrepresented."[9] But whether the ideas are truly Taylor's or not, there is no question that plenty of companies have practiced "Taylorism" in its worst form. Our quarrel is not with those who find it objectionable, but only with the idea that it is inseparable from work measurement. These critics say that the whole idea of establishing a quantifiable work standard, which is necessary to determining a piecerate, can only mean treating people like machines; dehumanization and alienation in the workplace is the result. This criticism is, of course, applicable to many group incentive plans as well.

Ironically, the same critics don't seem to think that it is

---

[9]Peter F. Drucker, *Toward the Next Economics and Other Essays* (New York: Harper & Row, 1981), p. 101.

alienating and dehumanizing to use a stopwatch on a runner or to apply the concept of par to a golfer. But no doubt they would argue that the sports analogy does not apply. The golfer or runner has assented to the fairness of the standards, tries to use his or her intelligence and skill to exceed the standards, and, we assume, has voluntarily decided to play the sport in first place. Now, no work environment, whether it has piece-rates or not, can possibly guarantee the last requirement—that everyone will be there strictly for love. But it is in the interest of every company to try to fulfill the first two: to devise standards that people will perceive as fair and to so conceive the work as to give the widest possible scope for individual intelligence and initiative. Once that is done, then work measurement can lead to a greater sense of identification with one's work, as, by all accounts, it has at Lincoln Electric.[10]

How It Works

None of the above is meant to imply that individual incentives have no problems. To get a better idea of both the problems and the advantages, let's consider some examples.

Maytag may be a household word in this country, but few know the Maytag Company as a keeper of the flame regarding the value of individual incentive plans. In fact, the best known representative of the company, the "Maytag man" who makes repairs, is not on an individual incentive plan. The company's view is that it is too difficult to set standards for his work; only when he gets out into the field is it possible to determine how much time each repair job will take.

But a substantial percentage of his co-workers back at the plant are on individual incentives. Of the company's approximately 1,900 workers, about 55 percent work against a quan-

---

[10]One gainsharing company (wishing to remain anonymous) has taken the sports analogy literally. All its standards of performance, which happen to be tied to group incentives, are put in terms of baseball, with runs, hits, errors, home runs, and runs batted in.

titative standard. About 40 percent of these are on individual incentives; most of the rest, who are on group incentives, work on either the automatic washer assembly line or the dishwasher assembly line. The 45 percent of the hourly workers who are not on incentives do backup work with output difficult to measure against a direct standard. For instance, nonincentive workers include forklift drivers, whose job is to transport materials within the plant to places where they're needed; electricians, who are responsible for maintaining and repairing the plant's electrical systems; and other employees involved with such tasks as receiving and shipping, materials handling, machine setups, and maintenance. As with the Maytag repairman, it is difficult to set up some standard unit of time that it would take to perform any of these jobs; the nature of the tasks can change from day to day in unpredictable ways.

Another manufacturing company, Deere & Company, well known as a maker of farm equipment, has a very similar arrangement. At Deere about 45 percent of the hourly employees work against a standard, with most of these on individual incentives. The basic approach is the same as at Maytag— which is to define the work group according to the smallest possible human unit directly involved with turning out the product. This unit may be one person or, as on Maytag's assembly lines, large groups of people. The fact that both companies have many workers on individual incentives indicates that, contrary to popular belief, a lot of manufacturing work still can be defined on an individual basis.

The formula that both companies use is the one that is most commonly applied under piecework plans: the worker receives a bonus on a "one for one" basis. That is, if your hourly output is 10 percent above the standard, then you are paid a bonus that is 10 percent of your hourly wage; if it is 20 percent above the standard, then your bonus is 20 percent, and so on. In fact, both Deere and Maytag say that 35 to 40 percent above standard is the average performance of their people who are on incentives.

The philosophy, then, is to push the gainsharing plan as far down the ladder of our inverted pyramid as possible in order to achieve the maximum fit between individual incentive and reward. One result of this approach, as we have said, is that the gainsharing plan becomes selective: indirect labor does not get included. Of course, it is conceivable that in certain situations everyone's work will be susceptible to measurement, in which case all employees will be on individual incentive plans. But as a practical matter, this isn't very likely. For this reason, selectivity is almost an inherent part of individual incentive plans: An appreciable percentage of the employees will be left out. This has its disadvantages, but one clear advantage is that the companies can afford to be relatively generous to the favored few. If all employees got a share of the bonus pot, as they would under a group incentive plan, then there would be less to go around per person.

To see how this works, consider a nonmanufacturing company where individual incentives are a clearly accepted form of compensation: a Wall Street brokerage firm. A typical firm's labor force includes not just the brokers but a whole group of indirect laborers, including secretaries, securities analysts, and operations people. If the firm were on a group incentive plan, then bonuses from an increase in commission business would be proportionately distributed to everyone. But the firm assumes that the brokers crucially determine commission business. For this reason, although the firm might often grant yearend bonuses to everyone, it is the brokers who are the primary beneficiaries of the bonus pot.

Thus, companies on individual incentives can concentrate the extra dollars on the people whose discretionary effort matters most. But of course they pay a price for this advantage. Among other problems, there is the danger that the other employees, particularly the hourly people, will become disgruntled by the preferential treatment. Deere and Maytag remedy the imbalance by maintaining a higher base wage for the hourly workers who do not work on standards. In both companies, the base pay of these workers is 15 percent higher than the workers who are on gainsharing. So if these workers' upside potential is less—the average worker on gainsharing does take home more—their downside risk is also less. This disparity is even greater at Lincoln Electric, where, as we mentioned in the first chapter, the base wage for piecerates is technically zero, but where workers who are not on piecerates do receive a base wage. In addition, at Deere, Maytag, and Lincoln, people who are not on piecerates can apply for these jobs when they become available. Some workers, it turns out, would rather remain at a less-demanding, nonincentive job, particularly if the base wage is higher. So in the long run, the situation may sort itself out, with people ending up at the kind of job they prefer.

A related problem with selective gainsharing is that it does nothing to boost the discretionary effort of the indirect worker. Some companies deal with this problem by combining their individual incentive plans with a companywide plan for everyone. For instance, Wolverine Worldwide, Inc., a manufacturing company, has more than half its employees on an individual plan; it pays them an incentive bonus according to the same one-for-one gainsharing formula that is found at Deere and Maytag. But it also maintains all its employees on a companywide Scanlon plan. And as we've mentioned, at Lincoln Electric there is a profit-sharing and stock purchase plan for all employees in addition to the piecerates that cover about half of them.

One final point about companies that successfully maintain individual incentive plans: They all recognize that to update and maintain fair standards for every worker requires a substantial commitment of time and effort. By contrast, far less effort is required to maintain fair standards for group incentive plans. The unwillingness to spend this time and effort is the main reason why many companies have seen their individual incentive plans come to grief.

The Future of Individual Incentives

"The question of individual incentives has been settled in industry; the funeral was 20–25 years ago."[11] So writes a gain-

---

[11]Private correspondence from Mitchell Fein, January 1984.

sharing consultant committed to plantwide incentive plans. In the manufacturing sector, the trend has definitely been away from individual incentives although individual piece-rates still dominate such industries as men's apparel, hosiery, and footwear.[12] But the real issue is whether there are circumstances in which individual incentives can be successful. We have suggested here that this question is not settled, but open.

Individual incentive plans provide the maximimum fit between individual incentives and rewards; that is their principal strength. The potential problems are numerous, but a company that is determined to put in the time and effort can deal with them all. Ultimately the choice is a matter of managerial philosophy. A company may feel that whatever the benefit from individual incentives, in the long run the company will be better off if its gainsharing plan helps to foster a sense of mutual support that only a plantwide approach can bring. Or it may decide to straddle the two approaches by combining individual incentives with a plantwide approach, as in the cases we described above. Here the implicit philosophy is that while it is useful to concentrate the incentive bonus on those workers who have the most direct effect on output, productivity receives an added boost if there is also an incentive bonus for everyone.

The practical issue, which is whether there is a great deal of work that still can be defined on an individual basis, is really no issue at all. Companies that use individual incentives know their business well enough to be sensitive to this question. Accordingly, if individual incentives really were inappropriate, the companies simply wouldn't use them. That is why, as we have indicated, it's best to think of these companies not as believers in individual incentives as such, but as having an orientation toward defining the work situation in terms of the smallest human unit directly involved with the work: individuals when they make sense, large groups when they do.

---

[12]See Norma W. Carlson, "Time Rates Tighten Their Grip on Manufacturing Industries," *Monthly Labor Review*, May 1982, pp. 15–21.

That orientation may be particularly appropriate to the kinds of industries that remain relatively untouched by gain-sharing: those belonging to the service sector. To be sure, the service sector has some experience with individual incentives, since it does employ waiters, waitresses, and salespeople. But aside from profit sharing and employee ownership, which we will get to in a later chapter, gainsharing plans have mostly focused on the manufacturing sector. Of course, the main reason for this is that, unlike services, the manufacturing sector has a tangible product that is easily measured.

But within service organizations, there are functions that may well be susceptible to measurement. For instance, there are processes in many service organizations that are analogous to manufacturing. These might include check encoding at banks, the production of credit cards at financial institutions, laundry services at hospitals and hotels, and a whole series of functions involved with computers, including word processing, keypunching, and clerical tasks. It might be possible in these cases to set a standard and to pay a bonus to the extent that the standard is exceeded.

Other jobs, such as computer programming, might be susceptible to measurement in a different way. Once having received an assigment, the programmer would be asked to "bid" for it in the same sense that an outside countractor or consultant would. The programmer would negotiate an agreement according to which he or she would be commited to turning out an acceptable product within a certain number of worker-hours. In that way, a standard would be set. If the programmer exceeds the standard—delivers acceptable product before the agreed upon time—then a bonus would be paid. This "job shop" approach may be applicable to a whole range of functions that otherwise seem impossible to measure: research, writing, and almost any other kind of special project. The benefit to the company, of course, is that it would motivate discretionary effort: If standards are exceeded, then the employee would be able to complete more projects over the course of a year.

The point, then, is that service organizations might structure their payment systems in ways that resemble those of the manufacturing companies that use piecerates. Jobs that are measurable in either of the two ways that we have just described would be put on gainsharing. Jobs that are not measurable might receive a higher base wage in order to compensate people for the discriminatory treatment. Each work unit would be defined in any way that is expedient, anywhere from a single employee to a large group.

Regarding the latter issue, we note that while it is normally fashionable to talk about the increasing importance of the large group in the workplace, the press has recently been reporting the opposite trend—that of the single employee working at home. This practice has been variously called white-collar homework, cottaging, flexiplace, or telecommuting (when computers are used, as they often are). According to one forecast, within the next 10 years, millions of people will be working in this way.[13] The jobs that could be performed at home—including clerical tasks, computer programming, writing, and financial analysis—might turn out be suitable for individual incentive plans. In fact, that possibility has already occurred to Blue Cross/Blue Shield of South Carolina. It pays homebased employees on a piecework basis for the clerical function of punching paper claims into its computer system. According to the company, output per person among homebased employees is 50 percent greater than among the employees who do the same work from the office; in addition, the homebased employees' error rate is lower.[14]

In other words, the new age of telecommunications may give individual incentive plans a new lease on life.

---

[13]See, for example, Fitz K. Plous, Jr., "Flexiplace," *Across the Board*, July/August 1982, pp. 66–68, and "If Home Is Where the Work Is," *Business Week*, May 3, 1982, p. 66.

[14]Cited in Plous, "Flexiplace," p. 67; also based on November 2, 1983, conversation with George Johnson, the company's assistant vice president of communications.

"No member of a crew is praised for the rugged individuality of his rowing."

Ralph Waldo Emerson

Chapter 3

Group Incentives I: Physical Productivity Plans

The past two years have been a period of painful transition for the XYZ Company, a manufacturing firm located in the Midwest.[1] For about a decade, the company had been using the group gainsharing system known as the Rucker plan. But eventual dissatisfaction with the way that was working caused the scrapping of the Rucker plan and the introduction of an Improshare plan in its place. Then, problems with the way Improshare was going brought another reappraisal—followed by substantial modifications. The company now has a kind of Improshare hybrid which it believes will finally address its particular needs.

Throughout this process, the people at XYZ remained convinced that the problem lay with the method and not the concept; their idea was not to repudiate group incentives, but to find the right approach. And their experience underscores

---

[1]Company XYZ has asked that its identity remain confidential. Accordingly, in addition to suppressing the company's real name, we have altered certain minor details, none of which affect the basic account.

the fact that the right approach does not always come easily. Even within the limits of group incentives, the choices are not necessarily tame ones; consequences, not always pleasant ones, follow from each. Later on, we'll examine why Company XYZ made the choices it did. But first we need to understand the trade-offs that any company must consider before installing a group incentives plan.

The Inverted Pyramid Again

Just as you can place the four main categories of gainsharing on an inverted pyramid, you can also place on the same pyramid the two main categories of group incentives. Figure 3–1 shows a piece of our inverted pyramid under a microscope. What we have done is taken the group incentives rung and separated it into two parts, each of which represents a different horizon of responsibility. Small as these differences may look on a graph, their implications in human terms are quite important.

First on the pyramid are the physical productivity plans, of which Improshare (*Im*proved *Pro*ductivity through *Shar*ing)

Figure 3–1
The Hierarchy of Group Incentives

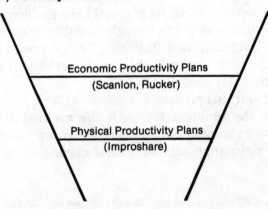

Economic Productivity Plans
(Scanlon, Rucker)

Physical Productivity Plans
(Improshare)

Horizon of individual responsibility for
financial performance of company

is a primary example. We might compare Improshare to a piecework plan, except that it rewards wage and salary workers as a group. Improshare's horizon of responsibility is the narrowest of the group incentive plans because it defines labor's input and output in physical terms. Just like a piecework plan, Improshare measures labor's input in hours and its output in physical units. In addition, there are many customized plans that use various physical indicators of performance, some of which we'll be describing later on.

One rung up on the pyramid are economic productivity plans. They broaden the employee's horizon of responsibility by defining labor's performance in dollar terms. For instance, the standard Scanlon plan formula depends on a ratio of labor costs to the sales value of production. While changes in physical productivity can affect this ratio, so can other factors beyond the direct control of most workers. Another economic productivity plan is the Rucker plan, which introduces even more financial considerations into the formula by including not just sales and wages but the dollar value of a whole range of other costs.

The Improshare formula is closest to the lowest rung on the pyramid, which is individual incentive plans; the Rucker and Scanlon plans are closest to the next-highest rung, which is profit sharing. Also, recall that at the lowest point on the pyramid there is a maximum fit between individual incentive and reward. A similar point applies to this segment of the pyramid: The fit between individual incentive and reward is greater under Improshare and looser under the Scanlon and Rucker plans.

We'll elaborate on these differences in this chapter and the next.

Improshare

Mitchell Fein, the creator of Improshare, is an industrial engineer with many years of experience—and with strong and clearly articulated beliefs. Those beliefs are well reflected in his Improshare plan.

Output per Worker-Hour

Fein's main point of departure is the idea that the large majority of workers prefer a narrow horizon of responsibility to a broad one. Accordingly, Fein thinks, a properly designed gain-sharing plan must concentrate solely on the factors that workers can directly affect. When it violates this principle, the gainsharing formula goes astray. Workers want neither responsibility for nor control over such financial variables as sales and costs of production. Those issues are the responsibility of management.

Thus, as we have said, the basic Improshare formula is similar to a piecerate formula except that it affects the entire organization. The plan generally covers all employees, both hourly and salaried. People normally excluded are senior management and others covered by a management bonus plan. The system determines a standard in terms of physical output per worker-hour and then pays workers a bonus to the extent that the standard is exceeded. Gains are usually calculated weekly and averaged out over a span of weeks to smooth out variations in the production cycle. Bonuses are normally distributed with each employee's paycheck.

To see how Improshare might work, take a simple example. Assume that the company turns out a single product.[2] In order to determine a standard, it is expedient to consider a full year's performance, so that high and low weeks can be averaged out. Say that average output per week has been 1,000 units in the recent 12-month period. Assume also that, over the course of the year, the average number of hours per week worked at the company—including all direct and indirect hourly workers as well as all salaried workers—was 4,000. That means each unit of output should require 4.0 standard worker-hours (4,000 hours divided by 1,000 units).

---

[2]The formula for a multiproduct plant is conceptually the same, although more complicated arithmetically. For an explanation, see Mitchell Fein, *IMPRO-SHARE: An Alternative to Traditional Managing* (Norcross, Ga.: American Institute of Industrial Engineers, 1981).

Now say that workers take 4,000 hours to produce 1,200 units of output in a given week. At 4.0 standard hours per unit, that level of output should take 4,800 hours (4.0 × 1,200). But since it actually took 4,000 hours, workers are saving the company 800 hours of labor time (4,800 − 4,000). Since the gains are split with the company on a 50–50 basis, workers' share of that savings is 400 hours (half of 800). To determine what this means in bonus pay, we simply take the 400 hours as a percentage of the actual hours worked: 400/4,000 = 10 percent. Each employee receives a 10 percent bonus in his or her paycheck. Profits, sales, or other costs of production clearly have no direct effect on this bonus. The employees have done their part, which is to improve output per worker-hour; management must do the rest.

Fein has both philosophical and practical reasons for preferring plantwide incentives over the kind we described in the previous chapter. Philosophically, he believes that "productivity improvement should be a companywide activity, with no we-they distinctions."[3] And as a practical matter, he stresses the difficulties of monitoring hundreds or even thousands of standards and the danger of demoralizing workers who are not on incentives. Under Improshare, the number of standards that has to be determined depends only on the number of final products, rather than on the number of workers who might be placed on standards. And since all workers receive the bonus, there is no issue of excluding people from the incentive program.

Two attributes of Improshare tend to make it more advantageous to employees than conventional piecework plans. First, as Fein puts it, "Traditional time standards are set by how long it 'should take' to perform certain tasks. Improshare standards are the average of how much time it 'did take.' "[4] As a practical matter, how long it did take tends to be an easier standard than how long it should. Second, under conventional

---

[3]Mitchell Fein, "Improved Productivity through Worker Involvement" (Hillsdale, N.J.: Mitchell Fein, Inc., 1982), p. 13.

[4]Private correspondence, January 1984.

piecework plans, increases in productivity that are due to improvements in methods and procedures generally bring a rise in standards. This happens even if the changes are initiated by the workers, a policy that can create a disincentive for workers to suggest such improvements. On the other hand, under Improshare, these improvements bring no change in the standards (although new capital equipment is another matter, as we'll see later). The gains from the increase in productivity are shared by workers in the usual way, even though these gains may be due to improvements initiated by management. Of course, there is nothing inherent in conventional piecework plans that would prevent them from adopting these two attributes of Improshare.

On the other hand, conventional piecework plans generally give participating workers a "one for one" share of productivity gains: a 10 percent increase in productivity brings a 10 percent bonus, a 20 percent increase brings a 20 percent bonus, and so on. By contrast, the Improshare formula pays on a "one half for one" basis, with a 10 percent increase earning employees a 5 percent bonus and a 20 percent increase earning a 10 percent bonus. Part of the reason companies with piecework plans can pay on a one-for-one basis has to do with a point we made in the previous chapter: since many workers are excluded from the bonus arrangement, these companies can afford to be generous to the favored few. Under Improshare, as we have mentioned, almost all employees participate in the bonus.

The Company's Share

Fein refers to his one-half-for-one Improshare formula as "50–50 sharing." The use of the phrase is proper, so long as we are clear on its meaning. To begin with, it of course does not mean that workers get 50 percent of the gains of increased output; that could happen only if labor costs were 100 percent of revenues, which would be impossible. Rather, it means that workers get 50 percent of the savings gained in worker-hours.

In the example we cited above, workers get half of the value of the 800 hours that the standard said they saved.

What about the company's share? To see how a company normally benefits from this formula, assume the same example as above of labor receiving a 10 percent bonus for producing 20 percent more output in the same number of hours (a rise from 1,000 units a week to 1,200). The costs to the company of producing the additional units decline for three main reasons. First, the 50–50 split means that payroll costs for these units decline by 50 percent; that is because labor receives half the usual rate for the additional output. Second, since the bonus is applied only to wages and salaries, the company saves on fringe benefits, which can often be quite substantial. And third, even if we assume that the 20 percent increase in output brings a proportionate increase in all other variable costs (materials, supplies, and so on), the fixed costs (principally plant and equipment) remain the same; therefore, nonlabor costs for the additional units also decline.

In other words, Improshare brings the company additional output at a substantially reduced cost. The effect of this on a company's bottom line can be dramatic. For instance, imagine that our hypothetical company is operating at just below breakeven with output of 1,000 units a week. So long as prices remain the same for additional output, the company may suddenly become quite profitable from the Improshare-induced increment of 200 units. Similarly, if the first 1,000 units already are being produced at a profit, then Improshare's effect will be to raise profits per unit on the additional output. In either case, the company's return on the Improshare bonus will be substantial.

Raising Standards

Another important component in the Improshare plan is what Fein calls the "buyback" provision. The buyback provision refers to the opportunity for management to raise the production standard—the standard against which output per hour is measured—by paying employees a substantial one-time bonus. Hence, by paying the bonus, the company "buys back" the old standard.

This provision addresses an important issue: labor's fear that management will raise the standards on them if they perform too well. One gainsharing company we interviewed (not on Improshare) admitted that this was a problem. There were employees at the company who would work until they produced to about 130 percent of the standard; then they would stop working for the rest of the day. It is possible that some of these people simply preferred that way of working, rather like the writer who quits for the day after he has produced his self-imposed quota of words. But the company was honest enough to admit that some people probably feared a raising of standards if their output was too high. Improshare's buyback provision addresses this problem. It permits the company to raise the standard, but at a price.

To begin with, the buyback of the standard becomes an issue only if performance is consistently exceeding 60 percent above standard. That is because of another rule affecting the weekly bonus; the rule sets a payout bonus ceiling that is generally set at the arbitrary level of 30 percent of earnings. Given the 50–50 split, this means that whenever performance exceeds 60 percent above standard, only a 30 percent bonus will be paid; the extra money will be held as a reserve against less-productive weeks. But if performance remains at better than 60 percent above standard, then the reserve will accumulate. The only way for it to be paid is through a buyback of the standard.

Accordingly, the buyback provision essentially works this way. Say that labor is performing at 80 percent above the standard. Then employees should be entitled to a 40 percent bonus (half of the 80). But under the 30 percent bonus ceiling rule, the extra 10 points flows into an ever-growing reserve. Now say that labor and management agree to raise standards so that 80 percent above standard will be treated as though it were 60 percent. In other words, they agree to take 20 points of credit away from the current number from which labor's bonus is computed. In accordance with the 50–50 split, this means that labor's weekly bonus will be reduced by 10 points (half of the 20). What the company must do is make a one-time payment to each employee that is equal to the annualized value of this 10 percent. For instance, to an employee earning a base of $400 a week, this 10 percent is worth a bonus check of $40 a week (.10 × $400). Since the agreement is to rescind the bonus by 10 percent, the company must pay the employee a one-time bonus of $2000 ($40 × 50, assuming a 50-week year). For all other employees, the calculation works out the same; the company must pay each a one-time bonus that is 10 percent of his or her annual base wage or salary.

Thus, the old standard has been "bought back." According to our example, the new standard requires in effect that any level of performance will be multiplied by 160/180 or .8889. Thus, for instance, what was formerly 180 percent of standard will now be treated as though it were 160 percent (180 × .8889); 170 percent of standard will now be treated as though it were 151.1 percent (170 × .8889), and so on. (In practice, the .8889 is multiplied by Improshare's standard number of hours required to produce a unit.) If the level of performance continues at what would have been 180 percent of standard, then future bonuses are effectively reduced by 10 points. But in return the company has had to pay all the bonus money that it would save for the first year.

Similarly, say that the buyback agreement is such that 180 percent will be treated as though it were 155 percent. Since this would mean an initial reduction of 25 points (180 − 155), the company would have to pay employees a one-time bonus of 12½ percent of their annual wage (half of the 25). Here again, the price is the annualized value of the company's savings. In this case, Improshare's standard number of hours will be multiplied by .8611 or 155/180.

The buyback can be arranged at any agreed-upon level whenever labor and management are convinced that performance will consistently exceed the arbitrary ceiling of 160 percent. Once the standard is raised so that performance will be at least slightly below the ceiling, then employees can begin to draw down the reserve that accumulated because of the ceiling.

Thus, the system compromises between the interests of the company and of the employees. Employees earn substantial rewards if they perform at better than 160 percent, but only on a one-time basis. The company gets to raise the standards, but only at a price. In a few cases, productivity has in fact gotten high enough for management and labor to exercise the buyback provision. But in all cases, what is more important is the knowledge that this agreement is in place; it should discourage any employee incentive to maintain informal quotas.

New Capital Equipment

As we have said, Improshare does not raise standards when there is an improvement in methods and procedures. But the installation of new capital equipment is another matter. Under these circumstances, there will be an increase in output per worker-hour clearly resulting from capital equipment that the company purchased. For this reason, it is only fair that standards be raised so that the company keeps these gains.

This is essentially what Improshare does, with one exception: It lets workers keep 10 percent of the gains attributable to the capital equipment, while giving the other 90 percent to the company. The company runs a "before and after" time study on the new capital equipment; in this way, it determines the effect the equipment will have on reducing the time required to produce a unit of output. It then uses this result to adjust the Improshare time standard so that workers are left with 10 percent of the potential gains. The company follows this procedure for any capital equipment worth $10,000 or more.

The effect of sharing at least some of these gains with workers is to get them to welcome capital equipment changes. If none of the gains were shared, then workers would perceive no benefit to themselves from such changes. But where there is a benefit, workers have an incentive to make the most of the increase in productivity that the new equipment permits.

Two Myths

A commonly held view about Improshare is that it is solely a labor productivity system—that it provides employees with no financial incentive for the more efficient use of other inputs such as materials, tools, and energy. While this is untrue, there is a truth involved.

As a practical matter, Fein usually does not advocate complicating the formula with other factors. It is hypothetically possible that under the standard Improshare formula, workers will have an incentive to waste materials and even to abuse their capital equipment if by so doing they can increase output per hour. But Fein maintains that such things do not happen if employees adopt a positive attitude toward the company and if managers do their job of properly overseeing the production process. In fact, Fein says that under Improshare, workers usually save on the use of other inputs without having to be offered a financial incentive to do so. He can cite plants where that very thing happened: After Improshare was introduced, fuel and compressed air use was reduced and maintenance supplies were saved, all through improved morale. In his view, the problems are rarely more subtle than that.

But whether Fein is right or wrong, the fact is that he has developed and applied Improshare plans that supplement the basic labor incentive with incentives of this kind. To the extent that employees are able to save the company money on materials and related costs, they can receive a bonus in addition to the bonus that rewards increases in output per hour.

Another commonly held view about Improshare is that it does not include greater employee involvement in decision making. Here again, this is untrue, although a truth is involved. Fein does urge that an Improshare plan include the creation of formal mechanisms for what he prefers to call "consultative managing"—"encourag[ing] worker involvement in day-to-day operations, in questioning how work is performed and suggesting changes."[5] Indeed, Fein's research, which we will be citing in a moment, shows that a company is likely to have greater success in boosting productivity when it combines an Improshare plan with mechanisms of this kind. But he candidly admits, and his research shows, that Improshare can also achieve success with traditional management techniques.

Track Record

Fein has done a follow-up of 72 companies that use Improshare. His main findings, summarized in Table 3–1, show that after one year the median gain in output per worker-hour was 21–22 percent. But note that the dispersion around the median is fairly wide, with 27 of the companies registering gains of 30 percent or better and 15 companies with gains of 10 percent or less. Thirty-four of these companies, or slightly more than half, employ unionized workers.

Also, notice the difference in performance between companies that installed productivity teams (problem-solving groups) and companies that did not. Many more of the companies without productivity teams are clustered at the low end of the scale. In fact, the median gain of the 52 companies with productivity teams was 25 percent versus a median of 15 percent for the 20 others. As we have mentioned, greater employee involvement in decision making is not necessary to a successful Improshare program, but it helps.

Customized Plans

So far we have been describing what critics of standard plans would call a "canned formula." Now it's time to consider some of the customized approaches. One good place to begin is with the system developed at the East Greenville, Pennsylvania, Division of Knoll International Inc., a manufacturer of

---

[5]Fein, "Improved Productivity," p. 3.

Table 3–1
Productivity Improvement Obtained in Improshare Companies

Company	Productivity Team	Gain after One Year	Company	Productivity Team	Gain after One Year
1	No	0%	37	Yes	22%
2	No	0	38	Yes	22
3	No	0	39	Yes	22
4	No	0	40	No	22
5	No	3	41	Yes	25
6	Yes	7	42	Yes	25
7	No	8	43	Yes	26
8	No	8	44	Yes	26
9	Yes	8	45	No	28
10	Yes	8	46	Yes	30
11	Yes	8	47	Yes	30
12	Yes	9	48	Yes	30
13	Yes	10	49	No	31
14	No	10	50	Yes	32
15	Yes	10	51	Yes	32
16	No	11	52	Yes	32
17	Yes	12	53	No	32
18	No	15	54	No	32
19	No	15	55	Yes	34
20	Yes	15	56	Yes	35
21	Yes	15	57	Yes	35
22	Yes	15	58	Yes	36
23	No	16	59	Yes	40
24	Yes	16	60	Yes	42
25	Yes	16	61	Yes	42
26	Yes	16	62	Yes	44
27	Yes	16	63	Yes	44
28	Yes	16	64	Yes	52
29	Yes	18	65	Yes	52
30	Yes	18	66	Yes	55
31	Yes	18	67	Yes	55
32	Yes	18	68	Yes	58
33	yes	19	69	No	65
34	No	19	70	Yes	70
35	No	20	71	Yes	70
36	Yes	21	72	Yes	75

Source: Mitchell Fein, "Improved Productivity through Worker Involvement" (Hillsdale, N.J.: Mitchell Fein, Inc., 1982).

office furniture. Like Improshare, Knoll's gainsharing plan is a plantwide incentive plan; also like Improshare, it bases its rewards on what are primarily physical rather than financial measures of performance. But there the resemblance ends.

Novel Measures of Performance

What is most striking about Knoll's gainsharing plan are some of its measures of performance. These include factors that we'd normally regard as means to an end rather than as ends in themselves.

The company makes employees eligible for an incentive bonus on a monthly basis. One determinant of this bonus is the quality and *quantity* of employee suggestions. To begin with, the company credits employees with a $75 bonus for every cost-saving suggestion that is submitted. Whether or not the suggestion is ultimately implemented makes no difference; all that is required is that it be about cost reduction. If the suggestion is approved—meaning that it was deemed appropriate for implementation—then it is credited with an additional $100. And if it actually does get implemented, it gets a final bonus of $150. So any cost-saving suggestion gets three possible "hits," with the first being virtually guaranteed.

The suggestion system can also boost the monthly bonus according to a "breadth of participation" measure. This measure is determined by the percentage of the plant's 1,100 employees who annually submit a suggestion covering any area of concern, again regardless of whether the suggestion is implemented. Thus, a higher bonus is paid if all employees submit just one suggestion rather than, say, half of the employees each submitting two.

As you might expect, Knoll employees produce a lot of suggestions; the rate per person is more than three times the national average for companies with suggestion systems.[6]

---

[6]R. J. Bullock and Patti F. Bullock, "Gainsharing and Rubik's Cube: Solving System Problems," *National Productivity Review*, Autumn 1982, p. 405.

And as you might or might not expect, the system's rate of return is more than 400 percent. That is, the most recent data show that in the first nine months of 1983, the annualized savings resulting from the suggestions were four times the cost of all bonuses paid for the system.[7] These costs include the participation bonus, which as we've said is not specifically geared to cost saving. Perhaps because all suggestions must be signed, no one has taken advantage of the system by submitting frivolous suggestions. As with all gainsharing indicators at Knoll, suggestions are rewarded on a plantwide basis; individual employees who submit suggestions boost the bonus for everyone, not just for themselves.

Skeptics might wonder whether it really pays to reward employees regardless of whether their ideas become usable. Wouldn't it be more cost effective to award bonuses only for those ideas that are implemented? On the other hand, it may be that the approach is prompting people to come forward with usable ideas who wouldn't otherwise feel encouraged to do so.

Also, any short-term calculation misses the possibly far more important long-term benefits of the system. The company is telling its people: We want to pay you to think; the more you do it, the better you're likely to get at it; so even if your ideas aren't usable now, they may become usable later on.

In keeping with that philosophy, not only does Knoll pay bonuses for making suggestions, it pays bonuses for having meetings. "Action teams," to which every employee belongs, can boost the monthly bonus simply by having one meeting per month in which suggestions are discussed. Also, departments boost the monthly bonus by having one meeting per

---

[7]According to company records, in the first nine months of 1983, they paid $56,000 in bonuses for suggestions that yielded $230,000 in net annualized savings. That yields a better than fourfold return (230,000/56,000). The $56,000 figure also includes $10,000 in bonuses for having meetings at which suggestions are discussed. The net savings figure ($230,000) was computed by taking gross annualized savings ($295,000) minus the one-time cost of implementing the suggestions ($65,000). Most of the gross savings is recurring rather than one-time.

month in which department heads communicate company plans.

In addition to these indicators emphasizing means, Knoll applies several other measures of performance that emphasize results, some of which are also quite novel. For instance, one indicator that affects the monthly bonus is their measure of product quality. This is defined as a "return rate," which is computed by taking the dollar value of monthly returns as a percentage of the dollar value of monthly shipments. The monthly bonus is boosted to the extent that the return rate is lower than the predetermined standard of .5 percent. As the company writes in their gainsharing manual, "If an item is returned to Knoll for any reason whatsoever, it tells us that we have not satisfied our customers' needs." In the month of August 1983, the return rate was .4 percent. This 10th of a point improvement over the standard boosted the monthly bonus by $10,000.

Apart from the quality measure, the monthly bonus is affected by four quantitative measures of performance, all of which are variations on the theme of conventional productivity. One is called "plant performance," which is essentially a measure of output per worker-hour on the factory floor. A second is a "shipments goal," a measure of the amount of goods shipped from the plant in a given month. A third is a measure of "on-time deliveries . . . the number of times Knoll meets its shipping commitments." The fourth is a measure of "inventory turns . . . how many times a year we can sell the inventory we have on hand."[8]

Finally, Knoll has what it calls the Theme of the Quarter— any area that the company temporarily declares to be in need of improvement; better performance in that area provides a means of boosting the monthly bonus during the three months that the theme is in force. Themes of the quarter have included the controlling of scrap, the generating of cost-saving

---

[8]Quotations are from Knoll's manual on gainsharing. A full description of all measures of performance is available from Knoll International, Water Street, East Greenville, Pa. 18041, Attn: Thomas J. McCann, Director of Personnel.

suggestions for the manufacture of three new products, and reducing lost employee time due to accidents. The company also regards themes of the quarter as trial balloons for potential inclusion in the permanent set of formulas that determine the monthly bonus.

Complexity versus Simplicity

Clearly, a crucial difference between Improshare and Knoll's homegrown product is that one is simple and the other is less so. For instance, Improshare does not provide a quality measure, except indirectly. Since workers are credited only for output that meets the company's standards, and are debited for output that is returned by the customer, the assumption is that they already have a built-in motivation to maintain high quality. Similarly, Improshare applies only one measure of productivity; from Fein's standpoint, such things as a shipments goal and an on-time deliveries goal will either take care of themselves or are the responsibilities of management.

There should, of course, be a bias in favor of simplicity in any organization; all other things being equal, it is better to keep things simple than to make them complex. But sometimes other things aren't equal. At Knoll, simplicity is one criterion that they explicitly used to develop their measures of performance; but their judgment of their own situation led them to develop several measures rather than one. Or consider another case in point. We began this chapter by mentioning a company (called "XYZ" to maintain its anonymity) that replaced its Rucker plan with an Improshare plan and then modified the Improshare plan. Later on, we'll talk about their transition from Rucker to Improshare. Here we'll focus on what they did with their Improshare plan.

Company XYZ stands about midway between the relative complexity of Knoll and the simplicity of the standard Improshare plan. An Improshare output-per-hour standard still determines most of the company's incentive bonus. But the company has taken the view that other components would also help. Accordingly, workers now earn bonuses for conserving energy, operating supplies, and scrap metal. In each case the use of these inputs is put in ratio to pounds of output so that a standard can be determined. Beating the standard earns employees a bonus that is equal to 10 percent of the company's saving. Finally, the company also sets a shipments standard of 5 million pounds of product per month. Employees earn an extra bonus if more than that amount is shipped.

While bonuses based on conserving energy, operating supplies, and scrap metal are essentially within the limits of Improshare as it is conventionally defined, the bonus based on a shipment goal is not. We might ask, why have a shipment goal if the plant is already producing high output according to the basic Improshare formula? Won't there be a built-in tendency for more to be shipped if more is produced?

The company's answer is that the addition of the shipment goal may not be absolutely necessary, but it helps. Shipments are regarded as one link in the chain that could benefit from an extra incentive. The company takes a similar view with regard to the other added formulas. Since the energy conservation formula was introduced, the company has saved on energy by installing new lights that require less energy, by installing a boiler that runs on the plant's waste heat, and by seeing to it that space heaters are turned off earlier in the day. While incentive bonuses might not have been crucial to this process, they undoubtedly helped.

Perhaps the major lesson to be drawn is that a company should begin by keeping its gainsharing plan as simple as possible—but that it shouldn't hesitate to add other incentives if, over time, these seem warranted. On the other hand, it might see benefits in some of Knoll's more novel approaches right from the start; paying employees for suggestions might provide a valuable boost to morale.

Chapter 4

Group Incentives II: Economic Productivity Plans

In the previous chapter on group incentives, we considered *physical* productivity plans. Now we move one step up our inverted pyramid to examine plans that are tied to *economic* productivity.

To get a better fix on the difference between the two kinds of productivity, consider a couple of examples. Say that a group of workers turns out twice as many units as the year before in the same number of hours; their physical productivity has doubled. But now say that over the same period, the price the company can get for the product has been cut in half. In other words, the output of units per worker-hour has doubled, but dollars earned per worker-hour have remained the same. The result is that workers' economic productivity has not increased at all.

A similar difference applies to an increase in the productivity of other inputs. In the previous chapter, for instance, we

43

mentioned that Company XYZ paid workers an incentive for saving on energy. Say that the plant manages to reduce by 10 percent the number of Btu's consumed per unit of output. This means a 10 percent increase in the physical productivity of energy; and since the plant is on a physical productivity plan, it would reward its employees accordingly. But now say that over the same period, the price of energy has increased by 20 percent. In other words, while it takes less energy to produce a unit of output, it takes more energy dollars. So despite the increase in physical productivity, the economic productivity of energy has decreased.

The point, then, is that prices can decisively influence economic productivity even when physical productivity is moving in the opposite direction. That is why economic productivity plans belong on a higher rung of our inverted pyramid than do physical productivity plans; they broaden the employee's horizon of responsibility by taking market realities into account. One of the subjects of this chapter will be how companies deal with both the problems and opportunities that these market realities create.

The Scanlon Plan

"Folks ought to know we expect deficits no matter how much harder and smarter they work." The speaker is Tom Lester, the plant manager of Desoto Southwest in Garland, Texas.[1] The company, a manufacturer of paint products, has had a Scanlon gainsharing plan since 1970. The plan covers all personnel—managers, technicians, and hourly employees; the sole excep-

---

[1] This discussion of the Desoto plant is drawn primarily from Brian E. Graham-Moore, "Ten Years of Experience with the Scanlon Plan: Desoto Revisited," in Brian E. Graham-Moore and Timothy L. Ross, *Productivity Gainsharing: How Employee Incentive Programs Can Improve Business Performance* (Englewood Cliffs, N.J.: Prentice-Hall, 1983), pp. 62–88. It is also drawn from interviews with Brian E. Graham-Moore and with Robert Highland, personnel manager, Desoto Southwest.

tion is high level executives, who are on a special executive bonus plan. The formula that determines the monthly bonus is the classic Scanlon ratio:

$$\frac{\$ \text{ value of personnel costs}}{\$ \text{ value of production}}$$

Under the requirements of the plan, the company established a standard for this ratio, based on its past history. For instance, say that they determined a standard at 25 percent—that is, they found that over prior years, personnel costs averaged 25 percent of the dollar value of production. Now say that in a particular month the ratio is 24 percent, perhaps because of an increase in production, a decrease in labor costs, or both. Since the standard has been bettered, the company credits employees with a bonus, most of which it pays them and part of which it keeps in a reserve fund against deficit months. Deficits happen whenever the ratio exceeds the standard.

It was just such deficits that plant manager Tom Lester was referring to in the above statement. In most companies, when a plant manager says "we expect deficits," he means that the plant is going to lose money, but in a company with a gainsharing plan, he may mean something else. In this case, Tom Lester meant that the company's Scanlon plan was going to yield a negative bonus. Lester made the statement at a meeting of the company's "screening committee," a group of labor and management representatives who meet regularly to discuss matters of importance to company operations. He pointed out that during the approaching summer, the company needed to add workers to cover vacations, so personnel costs were going to rise. The result would be an increase in the numerator of the Scanlon ratio, which would in turn cause deficits in the employee bonus.

Under the rules of the plan, these deficits would have been much less of a problem to employees had they occurred in the early months of the year. The reason is that at the end of each calendar year, all accumulated reserves are paid out to em-

ployees. So if there is a deficit recorded in January, there is
nothing to charge it against; nor do the rules allow it to be
charged against future reserves. Under those circumstances,
then, there would still be no bonus, but the deficit would
disappear. Unfortunately, the deficits Tom Lester had in mind
were going to occur during the summer months, which meant
that they must be charged against reserves earned in prior
months of the year.

By speaking so honestly about the poor prospects for the
bonus regardless of workers' output ("no matter how much
smarter and harder they work"), Lester was making an important distinction between physical and economic productivity
plans. In effect, he was pointing to the broader horizon of
responsibility that an economic productivity plan like Scanlon requires of people. The employees responded to his comments not with complaints but with the suggestion that the
company hire fewer summer workers than usual, since higher
worker productivity should do the rest. The company implemented this suggestion, with the result that deficits were
reduced.

According to any indicator, the Scanlon plan has been
quite effective in boosting Desoto's productivity. In 1982, the
most recent year for which data are available, output per
worker-hour was 64 percent higher than in 1970, which was
the year before the Scanlon plan first started. Since there were
no major technological changes over this period, we may conclude that much or all of the increase was due to the Scanlon
plan. While there have been months of no bonuses, bonus
months have occurred in every calendar year. On a yearly
basis, bonuses have averaged from a low of 2 percent to a high
of 21 percent.

The formula used at Desoto was first developed in the
1930s by Joseph Scanlon, who was then research director with
the United Steelworkers. In a sense, the Scanlon ratio is the
basic Improshare formula with dollar signs on it. Where Improshare uses worker-hours, Scanlon uses labor costs; where
Improshare uses units of output, Scanlon uses output's dollar
value. The result is that market factors can alter the Scanlon

ratio. These include a change in selling prices: A price rise brings a higher bonus by increasing the dollar value of output, while a price decline brings a lower bonus by decreasing it. Similarly, a change in product mix between higher-priced and lower-priced goods can also alter output's dollar value and so bring a change in the bonus. All this can happen while output per worker-hour remains the same.

The Scanlon plan typically calls not just for gainsharing but for an elaborate employee involvement system to facilitate communication. In fact, some advocates of Scanlonism regard it as essentially an employee involvement system and only incidentally a system for gainsharing.

In any case, the Desoto experience indicates that employee involvement is absolutely necessary to the success of the gainsharing formula. Where the bonus is affected by market factors beyond workers' control, there need to be effective lines of communication so that people can appreciate what is happening. As Moore and Ross write in *The Scanlon Way to Improved Productivity*, "the philosophy of the plan encourages everyone to be involved with the product or service the organization produces." They add that "this philosophy and the involvement system tend to reinforce each other" as the individual "focuses attention on broader work areas and ultimately on the organizational objectives." The authors admit that employees "may not particularly like the negative changes, because everyone is still human, but they learn to understand and accept them better." They ask rhetorically, "What better way to learn about the economics of the business than to be actively involved as they are happening?"[2]

There are hundreds of companies that use gainsharing plans called Scanlon, but often their formulas are quite different from the one that Joseph Scanlon developed. As one consultant points out, the Scanlon label "has become essentially a generic term for nonprofit-sharing economic productivity

---

[2]Brian E. Moore and Timothy L. Ross, *The Scanlon Way to Improved Productivity* (New York: John Wiley & Sons, 1978), p. 6–8.

programs of all kinds."[3] In fact, "Scanlon" plans often resemble the other standard economic productivity program,
known as the Rucker plan, to which we now turn.

The Rucker Plan

We have suggested that the Scanlon formula is an economic
productivity version of the basic Improshare formula. In a
similar sense, we might say that the Rucker formula is an
economic productivity version of an Improshare formula that
includes incentives for saving on other inputs. The Rucker
plan is almost as old as the Scanlon plan, having been developed in the 1930s by economist Allan W. Rucker. Today the
consulting firm known as the Eddy-Rucker-Nickels Company
has exclusive control of the Rucker plan and title. The company has developed, installed, and maintained Rucker plans
at hundreds of firms nationwide.

The Formula

As we have said, the classic Scanlon formula measures performance against a standard of personnel costs in ratio to the
dollar value of production. The Rucker formula takes these
same two variables and introduces a third: the dollar value
of all materials, supplies, and services that the firm uses to
manufacture its product. Accordingly, the Rucker formula is
simply:

$$\frac{\$ \text{ value of personnel costs}}{\$ \text{ value of production} - \$ \text{ value of materials, supplies, services}}$$

Notice that this ratio is the same as the ratio we cited for
the Scanlon formula, except that now the dollar value of pro-

---

[3]Robert C. Scott, private correspondence, May 4, 1981.

duction has been "netted out" for the cost of materials, supplies, and outside services that the firm uses. In fact, the denominator has now become what economists refer to as "value added," so named because it expresses the *value* that a firm *adds* to a product. For instance, take a bakery that turns out bread. The difference between the market value of the bread and the cost of materials, supplies, and outside services used to bake the bread is the value the baker added. As we will see, the use of value added rather than the dollar value of production is precisely what builds into the formula the incentive to save on other inputs.

As with any gainsharing plan, a company using the Rucker plan must first establish a standard against which future performance is judged. The Rucker consultants recommend that the standard be based on several years of both good and bad market conditions. Say that a company looks at five years of its past performance and finds that on a monthly basis its key variables have averaged as follows:

Personnel	$ 30,000
Sales value of production	100,000
Materials, supplies, and outside services	40,000

According to our formula:

$$\frac{\$30{,}000}{\$100{,}000 - \$40{,}000} = \frac{\$30{,}000 \text{ (personnel costs)}}{\$60{,}000 \text{ (value added)}} = 50\%$$

Thus, our base period yields a standard ratio of personnel costs to value added of 50 percent. This means that, from now on, the company will apply a 50 percent standard to its monthly figure for value added. That 50 percent of value added will determine the dollars that labor is "allowed." These allowed personnel costs will then be compared with actual personnel costs. If there is a positive difference, then all of it will become the monthly bonus. If there is a negative difference—if labor is earning more than their 50 percent of value added—then this will count as a deficit.

For instance, say that value added has risen to $70,000, or $10,000 more than in our base period. Applying 50 percent to this number, we find that labor is allowed $35,000 (.5 × $70,000). Now say that personnel costs have risen to $33,000. The $2,000 difference ($35,000 − $33,000) is the bonus for the month. On the other hand, if personnel costs had risen to $37,000, then this would yield a $2,000 deficit ($35,000 − $37,000). As with most gainsharing plans, a portion of the monthly bonus is set aside as a reserve against deficit months. Of course, the worst that can happen from continuous deficit months is only that labor will earn no bonus; the deficits cannot be applied to base wages and salaries.

As we have explained, value added is equal to the sales value of production minus the cost of materials, supplies, and outside services. So if the sales value of production goes up by a dollar, value added goes up by a dollar; similarly, value added goes up by a dollar if the cost of materials, supplies, and outside services declines by a dollar. As for personnel costs, they become a factor in determining the bonus only after we have computed the costs that labor will be allowed.

These fundamental relationships crucially determine the results we get in the three examples cited in the addendum to this chapter. There we show the technically minded reader just how the Rucker arithmetic is affected by changes in the key numbers that determined our standard: personnel costs, sales value of production, and the cost of materials, supplies, and outside services. In the examples cited, we take the base-period numbers and vary each of them in turn while holding the other two constant. This tells us how the employee bonus is affected by an improvement in any one of them.

The results show first that out of every dollar increase in the sales value of production, labor gets 50 cents. That is because our standard is 50 percent. As our numbers indicate, if the standard had been 40 percent, labor would have gotten 40 cents out of every dollar; if 30 percent, then labor would have gotten 30 cents, and so on. The point, then, is that labor's share of an increase in the sales value of production is determined by the standard.

The same result applies to a decrease in the cost of other inputs—materials, supplies, and outside services: Out of every dollar saved on these inputs, labor gets a 50 percent bonus. Similarly, if the standard were 40 percent, labor would get 40 cents out of each dollar saved; if the standard were 30 percent, labor would get 30 cents, and so on. So here again, labor's share is determined by the standard.

Finally, with regard to a saving in personnel costs, we get a very different result. In this case, there is no sharing. For every dollar saved in personnel costs, labor gets a dollar. This 100 percent applies regardless of the standard percentage; labor gets 100 percent whether the standard is 30 percent or 50 percent. But in this case, we should emphasize the Rucker plan's two-edged sword: For every dollar increase in personnel costs, the bonus declines by a dollar. For instance, all raises and all increases in benefits erode the bonus on a one-to-one basis.

Excluded Costs

We see, then, that the Rucker formula gives the same weight to a dollar saved on materials as it gives to a dollar increase in sales. That is one characteristic that sets it apart from most other gainsharing plans; another is the broad range of variables to which the Rucker formula is sensitive. But there are still a lot of items in the company's financial picture that cannot affect the Rucker bonus. These include property taxes, income taxes, rent, charitable contributions, and the cost of equipment depreciation. Also, the personnel-costs category generally excludes the salaries of top-level personnel; the feeling is that this is one part of personnel costs that should not affect the bonus, since it is a cost over which labor has little control.

Finally, the Rucker bonus is not directly affected by profits. Of course, given the nature of the formula, profits and bonuses will be highly correlated in most cases. But if other costs not affecting the formula are increasing, it is still theoretically possible for high bonuses to be paid while profits are down.

The Two-Way Street

We've shown how employees can earn bonuses at different rates depending on which variable shows an improvement. But as we've indicated, and as the Eddy-Rucker-Nickels Company is the first to point out, just as each of these formulas can give, it can also take. Adverse moves in any of the three variables that affect the bonus can offset positive moves in the others. Thus, according to our example, the bonus will diminish by 50 cents from a dollar decrease in the sales value of production—and by 50 cents from a dollar increase in the cost of materials, supplies, and outside services. Also, a dollar increase in personnel costs will diminish the bonus by a full dollar. The result may be not a bonus but a deficit.

Robert C. Scott of the Eddy-Rucker-Nickels Company lists the following among factors that could increase personnel costs and so reduce the bonus at the rate of 100 percent on the dollar:[4]

> All future wage increases.
> All future salary increases.
> Cost of training new people during an expansion.
> Wage and salary costs necessary to comply with EPA and
>   OSHA regulations.

Scott also lists the following among factors that could increase the cost of materials, supplies, and outside services. As

---

[4]Robert C. Scott, "Exploring the Two-Way Streets of Economic Productivity Incentives" (Eddy-Rucker-Nickels Company).

we have said, increases of this kind reduce the bonus at a rate that is determined by the standard percentage:

Absorbed material cost increases.
Absorbed supply cost increases.
Absorbed costs for purchased services.
Special contractors coming in (example: electrical maintenance).

Finally, Scott lists "price reductions on products" as reducing the sales value of output. This, too, reduces the bonus at a rate that is determined by the standard percentage.

Scott comments that after studying the list, "your quick reaction may be to throw up your hands and say 'it can never work,' but go back and review each of these listings, remembering that nearly every item *is a two-way street* [italics his]." In other words, if there is a possible loss, there can also be a possible gain.

Physical Productivity versus Economic Productivity

You are absolutely correct that economic factors beyond your control were major reasons for the Rucker Plan not developing extra income for your people in recent times. The Plan was deliberately designed to reward superior *economic* productivity above that necessary to balance off regular pay and benefit increases. It *was not* designed to develop bonuses regardless of current economic conditions. That can happen only at the expense of your profitability and at the expense of your stockholders [italics in original].

So writes G. D. Sargent, president of the Eddy-Rucker-Nickels Company, in a letter addressed to an executive at Company XYZ. As we mentioned in the previous chapter, this was the company that had abandoned its Rucker plan in favor of an Improshare plan. The company felt that the the Rucker plan had worked well for a number of years. But a combination of higher wages and lower prices had recently been producing negative bonuses despite the fact that physical productivity had been increasing. So it decided to shift to a physical productivity plan.

In his letter, Sargent agrees that "physical productivity measurement may well develop bonuses," but only because "that approach ignores product prices, material costs, and wage increases." He adds that "most of our prospects for Rucker plans have been companies whose . . . physical productivity incentive plans have been paying off just fine, while their profitability has been disappearing." He concludes: "It's a matter of philosophy, I guess, but if you are rewarding 'productivity increases' while profits are going down, is that the best approach?"

At the company's invitation, Improshare's creator Mitchell Fein wrote a response to Sargent's letter. Fein writes:

> Rucker expects workers to overcome wage increases by increased productivity, which is not realistic. Theoretically wage increases are offset by increased sales prices, but competition and depressed business conditions may depress prices.

Fein goes on to defend the idea of paying workers bonuses for increased output per hour even when a company is losing money. He argues that such bonuses do not, as Sargent says, come out of shareholder income. An increase in physical productivity reduces the company's losses; therefore, the Improshare bonus is simply a sharing in the gains of that loss reduction.

Fein then goes on the offensive: "I'm inclined to turn Sargent's arguments upside down and ask why the company should share increased profits with employees when these are obtained by increased prices or increased business volume."

Company XYZ is still on a physical productivity plan and is reportedly quite happy with it. Meanwhile, hundreds of other companies continue to maintain Rucker plans—and continue to claim that their productivity has been boosted as a result.

Addendum: Calculating the Bonus under the Rucker Plan

The numbers that follow will be keyed to the base-period example on page 49. That is:

Personnel	$ 30,000
Sales value of production	100,000
Materials, supplies, and outside services	40,000

Example 1

Let's say that in a given month, the sales value of production rises by $10,000 while the other two variables remain the same. That is:

Personnel	$ 30,000
Sales value of production	110,000 (formerly $100,000)
Materials, supplies, and outside services	40,000

Now we'll follow the steps that are necessary to compute the bonus.

1. *Calculate value added.*

Value added =
$ value of production − $ value of materials, supplies, and outside services =
$110,000 − $40,000 =
$70,000 (formerly $60,000)

2. *Multiply value added by the standard in order to get allowed labor costs.* According to our standard, labor is entitled to 50 percent of value added:

Allowed labor costs =
.5 × $70,000 =
$35,000

3. *Subtract actual labor costs from allowed labor costs in order to compute the bonus.* Recall that actual labor costs are $30,000:

> Bonus =
> Allowed labor costs − Actual labor costs =
> $35,000 − $30,000 =
> $5,000

So the monthly bonus becomes $5,000, or 50 percent of the $10,000 increase in the value of production.

Example 2

Now say that in a given month, the value of materials, supplies, and outside services declines by $5,000 while the other two variables remain the same. That is:

Personnel	$ 30,000
Sales value of production	100,000
Materials, supplies, and outside services	35,000 (formerly $40,000)

Now we'll follow the same three steps that are necessary to compute the bonus.

1. *Calculate value added.*

> Value added =
> $100,000 − $35,000 =
> $65,000 (formerly $60,000)

2. *Multiply value added by the standard in order to get allowed labor costs.*

> Allowed labor costs =
> .5 × $65,000 =
> $32,500

3.   *Subtract actual labor costs from allowed labor costs in order to compute the bonus.*

Bonus
$32,500 − $30,000 =
$2,500

So the monthly bonus becomes $2,500, or 50 percent of the $5,000 decrease in materials, supplies, and outside services.

Example 3

Now take the final case: a saving on personnel costs. Say that personnel costs decline to $27,000 while the other two variables remain the same. That is:

Personnel	$ 27,000 (formerly $30,000)
Sales value of production	100,000
Materials, supplies, and outside services	40,000

Now we'll follow the same three steps.
1.   *Calculate value added.*

Value added =
$100,000 − $40,000 =
$60,000

2.   *Multiply value added by the standard in order to get allowed labor costs.*

Allowed labor costs =
.5 × $60,000 =
$30,000

3.   *Subtract actual labor costs from allowed labor costs in order to compute the bonus.* Recall that in this case, actual labor costs are $27,000:

> Bonus =
> Allowed labor costs − Actual labor costs =
> $30,000 − $27,000 =
> $3,000

So the monthly bonus becomes $3,000, or 100 percent of the $3,000 saving in personnel costs.

To see how deficits can arise, assume an adverse move in each case. In the first case, assume a decrease of $10,000 in the value of production (to $90,000); the result will be a $5,000 deficit. In the second case, assume an increase of $5,000 in the cost of materials, supplies, and outside services (to $45,000); the result will be a deficit of $2,500. In the third case, assume an increase of $3,000 in personnel costs; the result will be a deficit of $3,000.

"More than one hundred years ago, Abe Lincoln signed the Homestead Act making it possible for our people to own land. . . . The Homestead Act set the pattern for American capitalism. . . . Now we need an industrial Homestead Act, and that isn't impossible. As a matter of fact, any number of companies and corporations have tried in a variety of ways to spread ownership to their employees."

Ronald Reagan (radio broadcast, February, 1975)

Chapter 5

Industrial Homesteading: Profit Sharing and Employee Ownership

In an earlier chapter, we called individual incentive plans the stepchild of gainsharing. We could say the same about profit sharing and stock ownership. Specialists in gainsharing generally believe that these are ineffective ways of motivating discretionary effort. For instance, gainsharing consultant Carla O'Dell writes that "profit sharing plans tend to be weak motivators":

> Profit is affected by so many conditions beyond the control of the worker that it can rise when productivity is declining—and vice versa. There is often no connection, direct or otherwise, between effort and reward for most employees.[1]

---

[1]Carla O'Dell, *Gainsharing: Involvement, Incentives, and Productivity* (New York: American Management Association, 1981), p. 22.

O'Dell has a point worth considering. In our previous chapter, we spoke about the potential pitfalls of the broadened horizon of responsibility that is inherent in economic productivity plans like Rucker; too much of the workers' bonus becomes dependent on factors beyond their control. But profit sharing and stock ownership go the Rucker plan one better. Gains from either one are directly dependent on the bottom line.

At worst, we might say profit sharing and stock ownership impose on the worker a form of responsibility without power. Profits crucially depend on the strategic decisions of top management, and workers' ability to influence those decisions is minimal. By tying worker bonuses to profit performance, the company is asking workers to take responsibility for management decisions. On that basis, these forms of gainsharing may be appropriate for top management—and as is well known, they are often restricted to that level. But we might question their effectiveness in motivating the discretionary effort of anybody below that level.

Yet granting all that, there is still a plausible case to be made for these approaches under many circumstances. To begin with, as numerous studies have shown,[2] profit sharing and stock ownership are likely to have at least some positive effect on worker productivity, even at the lowest levels of decision making. Second, they are closely connected to a company's ability to pay; gainsharing plans further down on our inverted pyramid do not have this advantage. Third, as we'll see later on in this chapter, apart from the desire to boost productivity, there are other compelling reasons to offer profit-sharing and stock ownership plans. And fourth, there is no forced choice among the various forms of gainsharing. A company might find it useful to combine profit sharing and stock ownership with

---

[2]Apart from the NYSE survey discussed in our first chapter, see Michael Conte and Arnold S. Tannenbaum, "Employee-Owned Companies: Is the Difference Measurable?" *Monthly Labor Review*, July 1978.

other kinds of gainsharing plans, as one prominent advocate of profit sharing advises.[3]

Finally, under the right circumstances, profit sharing and stock ownership can serve as powerful motivators of discretionary effort. The key is to create an environment in which workers strongly identify with the goals of the company. For example, take a look at the case of Lincoln Electric in Cleveland, Ohio.

Lincoln Electric

In our first chapter, we called Lincoln Electric the Mount Everest of gainsharing. If that label is correct, then it alone is reason to take a closer look at this extraordinary company.[4]

Begin with the most pertinent fact: Lincoln's rate of productivity. According to an independent evaluation, the company's output per worker-hour is *two-and-a-half to three times greater* than at similar manufacturing firms turning out similar products.[5] This rate of productivity is of a piece with other facts amply documented about Lincoln: its low prices, low costs of production, and high rates of profit. The company has achieved this performance with what may be the most lightly supervised work force in the country; as we mentioned in an earlier chapter, they have approximately one supervisor for every 100 workers, compared with one for every 10 to 25 at most other companies.

---

[3]See the writings of Bert Metzger, president, Profit Sharing Research Foundation. These are available by writing the foundation at 1718 Sherman Avenue, Evanston, Illinois 60201.

[4]This material is drawn from James F. Lincoln, *Incentive Management* (Cleveland, Ohio: Lincoln Electric Company, 1951); also drawn from Richard S. Sabo, "What Is the Lincoln Incentive Management System?" (Cleveland, Ohio: Lincoln Electric Company, February 1983), and from interviews with Mr. Sabo, who is now Lincoln's manager of educational services.

[5]From a confidential study done by another manufacturing company interested in evaluating Lincoln's management methods.

Nature versus Nurture

How does the company do it? According to one view, Lincoln's secret lies in hiring the right people. This view holds that Lincoln's employees are 2,600 of the elite of this country: self-reliant, hardworking types who come to Lincoln with the full potential to involve themselves in all that the company stands for. In other words, it isn't so much Lincoln's system that nurtures these qualities in people; the qualities are already in their nature. And if that is true, it might also follow that if Lincoln employed more ordinary people, the company's performance would not be nearly as good.

There must be at least some truth in this view. A company that pays its employees as well as Lincoln does will tend to attract and hold good people. And since Lincoln has been paying extremely well for decades, over time it must have accumulated a work force of better-than-average ability. But of course, the company had to be successful to begin with in order to pay that well. So we are still left wondering whether, at some point in its past, Lincoln had an ordinary work force with which it was able to do extraordinary things. Also, when we consider the almost 3-to-1 gap in productivity between Lincoln and other companies, it becomes difficult to believe that Lincoln's people could be that much above average. Maybe the company's incentive management system also plays a role. That system, now decades old, is almost as striking as the company's unusual performance.

The Yearend Bonus

As we mentioned in the first chapter, about half the company's 2,600 employees are on a "zero-based" piecework system according to which people are rewarded only for what they produce that is of acceptable quality. By contrast, most other manufacturing firms with piecework plans tie performance to a bonus that is paid over and above a guaranteed base wage.

Lincoln's piecework system operates in direct conjunction

with the company's system of paying yearend bonuses, which is in all essential respects a form of profit sharing. The bonus system affects all employees with the exception of the chairman and the president, who are on a gainsharing plan of their own: Their salaries are wholly dependent on annual sales. The company does not call the bonus system profit sharing, because the system also includes a merit rating that affects each employee's profit share. The use of the merit rating does distinguish their system from conventional profit-sharing plans. But what distinguishes it even more from conventional profit sharing is the enormous bonuses that it pays out.

The bonus system works as follows. At the end of each year, the company takes out of pretax profits that portion that is left after setting aside stockholder dividends, reinvested earnings, and taxes. It then calculates what percentage this amount is of all wages and salaries and applies the percentage to each employee's base pay. The resulting figure, modified by the employee's merit rating, yields his or her bonus.

In other words, for each employee, the bonus formula is:

$$\text{Bonus} = \text{Base pay} \times \text{Merit rating} \times \text{Bonus percent}$$

The merit rating is calculated in points, ranging usually between .80 and 1.20. For example, say that the employee's wage is $20,000, the merit rating is 1.00, and the bonus percentage is 100 percent. Then:

$$\text{Bonus} = \$20,000 \times 1.00 \times 1.00 = \$20,000$$

So the bonus would be $20,000, or 100 percent of the wage. Now say that the employee's merit rating is 1.10. Then:

$$\text{Bonus} = \$20,000 \times 1.10 \times 1.00 = \$22,000$$

Thus, with a higher merit rating, the bonus becomes $22,000, or 110 percent of the wage.

These numbers are not hypothetical. In recent years, median pay for workers on piecerates has in fact been at approximately $20,000, and the bonus percentage has averaged 100 percent. This combines to total income of approximately $40,000 for each of these workers.

With a bonus as high as 100 percent, there is a substantial multiplicative effect—both down and up—that the formula can have on the income of a worker who is on piecerates. To see how this works, take the first example cited above. If a worker on a piecerate had managed to earn $21,000 in base pay rather than $20,000, then the merit rating of 1.00 and the bonus percentage of 100 percent would yield an extra $1,000 in bonus income:

Bonus = $21,000 × 1.00 × 1.00 = $21,000 (formerly $20,000)

Total income (base pay + bonus) would then be $42,000 ($21,000 + 21,000), or $2,000 higher than it would otherwise have been. On the other hand, if the same worker had earned $19,000 in base pay rather than $20,000, then the same formula would mean $1,000 less in bonus income:

Bonus = $19,000 × 1.00 × 1.00 = $19,000 (formerly $20,000)

Total income would then be $38,000 ($19,000 + $19,000), or $2,000 less than it would otherwise have been. In other words, under these quite normal assumptions, the total income effect of earning a dollar more or a dollar less is two for one.

The Stock Purchase Plan

Lincoln's employees have another way of sharing the gains of company performance: through ownership of the company's stock. Lincoln permits employees who have been with the company for one year or more to buy shares at book value, which is cheaper than the market value. Employees who want to sell their shares must sell them back to the company at the current book value price. Also, when employees leave the company, they must sell their shares back. Voting rights and dividends are the same as for stock that is owned by outsiders.

Approximately 75 percent of Lincoln's employees have taken advantage of this opportunity; they now own more than 40 percent of the company's stock. Employees earn price appreciation on the stock based upon the company's increases in book value; they also earn dividends, which are paid quarterly and which run at an annual rate of about 8 percent of the book value price. Employee demand for the company's stock chronically exceeds the supply. In order to deal with this problem, Lincoln has a policy of buying company stock from outsiders whenever it is available and then selling it to employees who want it.

Given the voluntary nature of the stock purchase plan, we must regard it as more than just a gainsharing plan. It is in itself an indication of the employees' willingness to participate in the fortunes of their company.

Guaranteed Employment

Most of us know something about the lifetime employment guarantee offered by certain Japanese corporations. Later on in this book, we'll make some points about this practice that are not so well known: that in bad times, the companies do lay off large numbers of their employees who have only temporary status; and that even the "lifetime" employees who are nonmanagerial must retire once they are 55 to 60 years old (see Chapter 6).

By contrast, Lincoln Electric has a guaranteed employment system that is more meaningful. First, the company has no mandatory retirement age. Second, it offers continuous employment to anyone who has been with the company for two years or more. Of course, the no-layoff policy does not exclude the right to fire people for inadequate performance. But if the company did this very often, it would have a much higher turnover rate than it does. Turnover is 4 percent a year, which is far below the average for most companies and which mostly involves people who leave voluntarily either to retire or to work at other jobs. It is also true that employees with less than two years' standing provide the company with a similar kind of buffer that Japanese companies get from temporary employees. But in fact, since 1958 when Lincoln first formally established the policy of guaranteed employment, they have had no layoffs whatsoever.

Certain other factors have helped the company avoid layoffs. First, there are the particulars of the commitment: The company does not guarantee a full-time job; it guarantees only that the worker can count on at least 30 hours per week of employment. Second, there is the gainsharing formula: Where the yearend bonus is such a large percentage of worker income, declining profits in bad times will mean a corresponding decline in the bonus.

These policies were put to the test in 1982, when Lincoln's business hit a severe downturn. Most companies would have responded to the situation with substantial layoffs. Lincoln laid nobody off, but it did manage to reduce its labor costs by approximately 25 percent from the year before. It achieved this, first, by putting its hourly employees on 30-hour weeks and, second, by reducing the yearend bonus. In 1981, a good year for business, the median base pay for workers on piecerates was $22,500 and the median bonus was also $22,500, which meant that median income was $45,000. In 1982, median income for workers on piecerates declined to $34,000, consisting of approximately $19,000 in base pay and $15,000 as a bonus. Of course, while this decline was steep, total income in 1982 was still at a level that is quite high for manufacturing workers generally. As of this writing, the 30-hour week has continued into 1983.

Despite the shortened hours, the company still found that there was not enough routine work to go around for all its employees. One of the ways it has used its surplus workers is to send them around the country to help sell the company's products. Lincoln has called this its "leopard" policy, so named for two reasons: first, because it was asking people to change their spots by becoming salesmen; and second, because it was sending them to those "spots" that had not previously been prospected. In 1983, the leopard policy brought the company an estimated $10 million in extra sales.

Job Security and Gainsharing

Lincoln's employment guarantee raises issues that have direct bearing on the success of gainsharing programs generally. To begin with, it is clear that Lincoln's guarantee serves as a powerful boost to worker loyalty. Of course, worker loyalty is important in any case, but it is particularly so in a company such as Lincoln that ties so much of employee income to profit sharing and stock ownership. The company is telling its people that it will not abandon them in hard times. And by all indications, the workers reciprocate: Morale through the past two difficult years has apparently remained high.

Other factors help, too. These include the company's involvement system: Every two weeks an "advisory board" of elected employee representatives meet with top management to discuss problems. They have the policy of promoting from within; almost all hiring is for entry-level jobs. And to be sure, there is also the relatively high payout that Lincoln was able to maintain even after it cut employee income by 25 percent. But this ability to pay so well is, in turn, due at least in part to the extremely high rate of productivity that the gainsharing system helps to motivate. In other words, the major elements of Lincoln's system tend to be mutually supporting. Just as the gainsharing system helps create a high rate of productivity, so the high rate of productivity helps create acceptance of the gainsharing system. Similarly, just as the flexibility in Lincoln's gainsharing helps the company live up to its employment guarantee, so the employment guarantee helps create a willingness to accept the flexibility in Lincoln's gainsharing.

The employment guarantee also does something else; it takes away workers' fears that higher productivity will mean the loss of their jobs. Why should they apply greater discretionary effort if all that they will get for their pains is unemployment insurance? This is an issue that we have neglected up to now, but one that has a direct bearing on all the gainsharing plans that we have discussed so far.

One point we should emphasize at the outset is that such fears appear to be less serious than we might normally think. The reason is simple: In many companies, where vulnerability to layoffs is a function of seniority, the majority of workers are fairly confident that the layoffs won't happen to them. In these cases, the only people who have real reason to fear job loss from higher productivity are the minority of relative newcomers.

Thus we have the sorry spectacle, in certain cases, of workers actually opposing job security for their fellows. In one company that maintained its workers on individual piecerates, the senior workers became concerned during a slow period that their piecerate bonuses would decline because of an insufficient amount of work; so they actually asked that the juniors be laid off. Similarly, Mitchell Fein has had no success with his proposal for a work-sharing modification of Improshare when companies are suffering a slowdown. His idea is that under these circumstances, both the company and the employees would contribute their share of productivity gains to a shortened workweek; the result would be lower incomes for workers, but the saving of jobs. Fein has gotten not a single company to accept the idea. The problem is not opposition from senior management—they generally support it—but opposition from the rank and file. Recall that even Lincoln Electric makes no formal job guarantee to the people who have been with the company for two years or less. The company's decision to keep these people on in bad times has meant that the other workers have had to accept a larger income cut than otherwise.

But even when the possibility of job loss does not threaten the majority of workers, it still poses a severe disincentive to the minority; and at times, the number of these threatened workers can approach a majority. Where a company's business is booming, the problem doesn't arise; if there is an employment effect from increased productivity, it will only be felt in the company's needing fewer new people. But in few cases is business always booming. That is why Lincoln's employment guarantee has a great deal to recommend it.

The Basic Approach

Can you argue with success? Of course you can—particularly when, as in this case, there is so much to choose from in explaining Lincoln's high rate of productivity. Lincoln's extraordinary performance may be primarily attributable to superior people, to superior management techniques, and to the piecerate system; it may be only marginally due to its profit-sharing and stock ownership plans.

But if a company does decide to institute such plans, then Lincoln's system does exemplify at least two basic guidelines that are useful to follow.

First, Lincoln clearly believes in applying other kinds of incentive plans in combination with profit sharing and stock ownership. In effect, it recognizes that there is no real substitute for the lower rungs of our inverted pyramid. As we have said, the company's piecerate system belongs on the lowest rung of the pyramid; on that rung there is the closest fit between individual incentive and reward. In addition, to go somewhat further up the pyramid, physical productivity programs such as Improshare are also quite compatible with profit sharing and stock ownership plans.

Second, the company has a whole set of policies aimed creating a sense of identification with the company: its policy of promoting from within, its involvement of employees in decision making, and its employment guarantee. Profit sharing and stock ownership can be a powerful motivators only to the extent that this sense of identification is strong.

Other Reasons

We began this chapter by saying that apart from boosting productivity, companies have other reasons for instituting profit sharing and stock ownership plans. The remainder of this chapter will be devoted to considering them.

ESOPs

"Under a communist government, the government owns everything including the people, and under what I advocate, the people own everything, including the government."[6]

These words were spoken by Senator Russell Long, an impassioned, inspiring, and highly effective advocate of worker capitalism in this country. Over the past decade, Senator Long has played a key role in pushing through legislation providing substantial tax benefits to companies that install employee stock ownership plans, commonly known as ESOPs.

ESOPs are different from the employee stock purchase plans that can be found at such companies as Lincoln Electric. As we'll see, they are adaptable to many uses. But in their essential form, they are stock participation plans that must, as a matter of law, cover most of a company's employees. The stock goes into a trust called an ESOT (for employee stock ownership trust). The trust allocates stock to each employee according to a formula; usually the amount of stock an employee gets is based on salary or on a combination of salary and length of service. Also, employees are subject to a vesting schedule, which means that there is a waiting period before they become entitled to their full allocation. Employees generally get their holdings in stock or in cash when they retire or leave. In return for giving stock to its employees, the company becomes eligible for different kinds of tax benefits. On

---

[6]Quoted in "Employee Ownership: A Symposium," held January 26, 1982 (Arlington, Va.: National Center for Employee Ownership), p. 5.

the other hand, because the stock going into the ESOT is in most cases newly issued, a cost imposed on the company is the dilution of its existing stock.

The leading theorist of ESOPs is Louis O. Kelso, the writer and lawyer who created the concept and whose ideas still provide the ESOP movement with its most widely cited ideological justification. Kelso's writings on employee stock ownership include *The Capitalist Manifesto* (written with Mortimer J. Adler), a book that is meant to be capitalism's answer to the more famous manifesto of Marx and Engels. The continued association of Kelso's ideas with the ESOP movement is unfortunate, since his core theory is a simple fallacy.

Essentially, Kelso believes that where the wages of labor are set by the laws of supply and demand, workers who do not own capital will earn income that is at or near subsistence levels. It follows from this that in a free labor market, workers must own capital if they are to get their share of the affluence that capital brings. Kelso bases his view of labor's true wage rate on an analysis of the physical productivity of labor compared with capital—what he has called his "two-factor theory." He points out that "capital instruments produce most of the wealth in an industrial economy" and that "labor in general produces only subsistence."[7]

These statements are essentially true when they bear on the relative productivity of capital and labor. Clearly, if all the country's capital equipment were suddenly to disappear, then everyone would be reduced to a subsistence level. But the statements have no bearing on the way wage rates are determined in a competitive economy. To begin with, owners of capital are not paid according to the productivity of that capital; they are paid according to the market system of profit and loss. It is true that in the short run, more productive capital can bring a rise in profits. But competitive forces make

---

[7]Louis O. Kelso and Patricia Hetter, "Man without Property," *Business and Society Review*, Summer 1972, pp. 17–18.

sure that "super normal" profits cannot persist for very long. If the capitalist down the street is earning a 30 percent profit, then you and I will be quite happy to take his business away by earning a 25 percent profit. We can put him out of business in either or both of two ways (a) bidding his labor away by offering higher wages and (b) charging lower prices (which raises real wages by making our products cheaper). From our standpoint, a 25 percent profit is a lot better than nothing, so it doesn't matter to us that we've destroyed our competition's 30 percent profit. And since we know that if we tried to earn 30 percent, we too would be vulnerable to being driven out of business, we contain our predilection for self-destructive greediness. The physical productivity of our capital has no direct bearing on these real-life considerations.

The point, then, is that if competition keeps profits down, then most of the rest of the economy's output will go to labor. And if the output of the economy is growing because of capital accumulation, then labor's income will grow as well. The market forces that determine this pattern will prevail in the future as much as they have in the past.

If Kelso were right in believing that workers get no share of the affluence attributable to capital accumulation, then this idea should have been confirmed a long time ago in wage rates. Current figures show that labor gets the overwhelming share of business income, but Kelso dismisses these figures on the grounds that today's wages and salaries are severely distorted by interventionist factors; in his view, these factors include unions, immigration barriers, minimum wage laws, and Keynesian full-employment policies. But he has much more trouble explaining the steady advance of wage rates when these factors were not present.

For instance, if Kelso's theory were valid, then the industrial transformation that took place during the second half of the 19th century and into the early part of the 20th should have shown no significant advance in labor's wage. Unionization and barriers to immigration were negligible; minimum wage rates and Keynesian full-employment policies were nonexistent; and most of the substantial increase in output was attributable to more and better capital. In fact, in almost every decade of this period, wage rates rose steadily; by 1916, the real hourly wage was approximately double what it had been in 1855.[8]

But if labor does not need stock ownership in order to avoid relative impoverishment, neither does the employee ownership movement need that kind of argument to justify its vision. The political, economic, and social benefits of giving people a direct stake in the fortunes of their company are real enough.

No less real are the tax benefits given to companies that install ESOPs. As we mentioned earlier, this is a key element in the ESOP legislation. One major tax benefit is the right to borrow money on terms that are extremely advantageous. Normally, when a company borrows money, only the interest is tax deductible. But if it borrows through an ESOP mechanism, then it can deduct both principal and interest. Take a simple example of a company in the top bracket of 46 percent borrowing $10 million. What the company must do is issue $10 million worth of stock in an ESOP trust (commonly referred to in this case as a "leveraged" ESOP). The company can then deduct this $10 million from its taxable income and thereby save $4.6 million in taxes (.46 × $10 million). The net result is that the company effectively repays only $5.4 million of the principal on the $10 million loan, with the other $4.6 million coming out of taxes that it would have paid anyway.

A different kind of tax benefit includes the right to claim a tax credit in return for creating an employee stock ownership trust—in this case, originally known as a "TRASOP" (Tax Reduction Act Stock Ownership Plan). TRASOPs were established by the Tax Reduction Act of 1975 and were based on a company's capital investment. President Reagan's Economic Recovery Tax Act of 1981 replaced TRASOP provisions with more liberal provisions based on a company's payroll—hence

---

[8]See figures cited in F. A. Harper, *Why Wages Rise* (Irvington-On-Hudson, N.Y.: Foundation for Economic Education, 1972), p. 11.

the term *PAYSOP.* Beginning in 1985, the equivalent of ¾ percent of a company's payroll will be eligible for the tax credit.

Because the PAYSOP offers a tax credit rather than a tax deduction, its tax benefits on a dollar-for-dollar basis are far greater than those of the leveraged ESOP. In the example we cited above, we showed that a company in the top tax bracket gets 46 cents subsidized by the taxpayer out of every ESOP dollar. But under the PAYSOP, the company gets a tax subsidy of 100 percent. On the other hand, the amount of stock that can be issued under a PAYSOP is tiny compared with a leveraged ESOP; and there are additional legal restrictions on PAYSOPs that are not imposed on other ESOPs. In any case, there is no forced choice; companies are free to take advantage of both PAYSOPs and leveraged ESOPs.

The ESOP mechanism provides tax benefits in other situations as well. For instance, take an owner of a closely held corporation who wants eventually to turn his shares into cash. Even if his company is quite profitable, he may have difficulty finding an outside buyer. Also, he may be reluctant to sell to an outsider if this means that the company he has built will not continue in its original form. An ESOP mechanism can provide a solution to his dilemma; he can sell his company to the employees. Under the ESOP arrangement, one tax benefit is that the owner is paid with tax-deductible company contributions rather than with after-tax employee savings. Another benefit is that the taxes the owner must pay on the sale are subject to preferential capital gains rates rather than ordinary income tax rates. Also, as we'll see later on, ESOPs are the preferred means of effecting employee buyouts of plants that would otherwise be closed by their parent company.

Given the tax benefits of ESOPs[9] and their potentially pos-

---

[9] A full-scale discussion of these tax benefits is beyond the scope of this chapter. For more information on ESOP tax benefits and for ESOP provisions generally, an excellent source is the ESOP Association of America, 1725 DeSales Street NW, Suite 400, Washington, D.C. 20036.

itive effect on productivity, it is hardly surprising that more than 5,000 companies have installed ESOPs. The wonder is only why more haven't done so.

Stock Purchase Plans

Despite the advantages of ESOPs, many companies (including Lincoln Electric) still use more straightforward stock purchase plans as a means of spreading ownership to their employees. Although there are plenty of exceptions, ESOPs generally bestow stock on employees. On the other hand, stock purchase plans by their very nature require that employees pay directly for the stock. A recent New York Stock Exchange survey found that more than 10 million people own stock that was acquired through purchase plans. For approximately 5 million of these, stock acquired in this way is the only stock they own. Among these 5 million, more than 35 percent own stock that is worth $5,000 or more, and almost 9 percent own stock worth $25,000 or more.[10]

Under many such plans, employees can conveniently purchase small amounts of stock on a regular basis, sometimes at a discount from the market price and usually without commission charges. As with ESOPs, companies can use stock purchase plans to raise money for capital investment. Some companies use stock purchase plans to supplement their ESOPs; other companies simply prefer stock purchase plans to ESOPs on the grounds that ownership is more meaningful when employees pay for it themselves.

On the other hand, stock purchase plans are not going to bring the kind of revolution in employee stock ownership that Russell Long is calling for. Senator Long has called stock purchase plans "the Marie Antoinette approach to expanded ownership": "Only instead of suggesting 'let them eat cake,' [the]

---

[10]See *Shareownership 1983* (New York: New York Stock Exchange, Office of Business Research, 1984).

recommend[ation is], 'let them buy stock.' "[11] Long is quite correct to point out that the majority of Americans simply can't afford to buy their company's stock to any significant extent.

As a Pension Plan

So far we mentioned the tax benefits of ESOPs and the capital-raising potential in stock purchase plans. As we have said, these are additional reasons for companies to have employee ownership plans, apart from the basic reason of boosting productivity.

Among the other uses to which both stock ownership and profit sharing can be put is to provide a pension plan for employees or to supplement the existing pension plan. Indeed, most of the approximately 350,000 profit-sharing plans in this country are set up partly for this reason; they are deferred profit-sharing plans, payable when the employee leaves the company.

From the company's standpoint, an advantage of tying all or part of employee pensions to these plans is flexibility; from the employees' standpoint, a disadvantage is uncertainty. If the company performs poorly, then employee pensions will be lower than otherwise; if it performs well, then employee pensions will be higher than otherwise.

Saving Jobs: Wage Concessions

> We can do nothing, and we can see our jobs drift overseas. Or we can create new patterns of relationships between management and employees. Our people are $30,000-a-year steelworkers. They may have to become investors, or risk losing their jobs.[12]

---

[11]*Congressional Record*, November 17, 1983, Part II, p. 10.

[12]Quoted in "The Labor Givebacks Are Spreading to Steel," *Business Week*, April 12, 1982, p. 40.

The speaker is an official of the United Steelworkers union. He was referring to the commitment they had gotten from the Wheeling-Pittsburgh Steel Corporation to deliver approximately $4,000 in preferred stock to each of its workers. This will match wage and benefits givebacks on a dollar-for-dollar basis.

People reading the front pages of the newspaper over the past few years would get the impression that profit-sharing and stock ownership plans serve one main purpose: as a quid pro quo for wage concessions. Ford, GM, Chrysler, Pan Am, and Eastern Airlines are among the better-known companies that have struck such agreements with their workers.

The logic of such agreements is clear: Companies facing increasing competition can afford to pay their workers at the old rates only if the company prospers. The solution is to give workers a piece of the action. Such gainsharing arrangements should also help motivate discretionary effort.

The more extreme form of workers getting a piece of the action—and thereby saving their jobs—is through employee buyouts. The story we tell in the next section is about one such case.

Saving Jobs: Employee Buyouts

The man speaking to the New York Stock Exchange interviewer was offering his view of Hyatt-Clark Industries, a manufacturing company based in Clark, New Jersey. The terms he used in describing the company were glowing. He spoke of it as an "extraordinarily powerful technical organization" with "the most advanced manufacturing processes in the world"; he added that the people at Hyatt had "enormous accumulated technical experience." In expressing his opinion, he was drawing on 35 years of experience in manufacturing, the last 6 with a prestigious consulting firm that had done a special study of Hyatt-Clark.[13]

---

[13]Tape-recorded interview with C. Douglas Howell, February 24, 1982. At that time, Howell was temporarily acting as president of Hyatt-Clark Industries, Clark, New Jersey.

There was an irony in what the man was saying—and it might have been amusing if it weren't so sad: Hyatt-Clark had come very near to being closed by what had formerly been its parent company, General Motors. GM had said that it was much more economical to buy from outside companies than to be supplied by their own subsidiary. But as our manufacturing expert attested, whatever was making Hyatt-Clark an albatross from GM's point of view—and threatening to turn it into a ghost town—could have had nothing to do with the technology of its plant or the skill of its workers. Luckily, the tragedy of a shutdown was avoided. Now GM is still supplied by Hyatt-Clark, but on a different footing: In 1981, GM sold the company to an ESOP.

In retrospect, it is clear that part of the company's problem had to do with worker motivation. Since the employee buyout, some divisions of the plant have had an unheard of doubling and tripling in output per worker. This quantum leap in productivity has mainly been the result of two factors. First, the union has agreed to the abolition of restrictive work rules. This has meant, among other things, that the same worker can tend more machines and that a number of jobs now deemed unnecessary could be abolished altogether. Second, there has been a huge increase in worker effort, a point that has been confirmed by one of the heads of the union local. He has said that before the worker takeover, "a lot of people were only working a few hours a day" but that now they were "pulling their weight, when they weren't doing it before."[14]

Hyatt-Clark is one of approximately 60 cases in which an employee buyout saved a plant that was about to be closed by its parent company; in all, about 50,000 jobs were directly involved.[15] In recent years virtually all of these buy-

---

[14]Tape-recorded interview on February 24, 1982, with James Zarello, shop chairman, Local 736, Hyatt-Clark Industries, Clark, New Jersey. The change at Hyatt-Clark has also involved greater worker involvement in decision making. For more on the connection between gainsharing and worker involvement, see Chapter 1.

[15]Cited in Linda Wintner, *Employee Buyouts: An Alternative to Plant Closings* (New York, The Conference Board, 1983), p. 4.

outs have been effected through the advantageous medium of the ESOP.

A common view holds that employee buyouts are generally a doomed attempt on the part of workers to hold on to their jobs. After all, if the managers in charge of the parent company couldn't make a go of it, how can you expect the employees to do so? This view is belied by the relative success of these companies: Of the estimated 60 cases, only two (quite small plants in both cases) have ended in financial failure.[16]

Nor should this relative success be especially surprising. To begin with, the very fact that these buyouts happened indicates that the workers were able to convince sources of outside finance that they could operate the plant successfully; the buyouts would never have happened if no outsiders had been convinced. Second, workers are generally willing to operate their own plants for lower rates of return than the parent companies expect. Third, buyouts often bring substantial wage concessions, as they did in the case of Hyatt-Clark. And finally, as the Hyatt-Clark case also indicates, buyouts can often create an upsurge in discretionary effort that was unheard of when the plant was owned by the parent company.

Fostering Democracy

"Drawing from our nation's 200 years of experience with political democracy at various levels of government, we can offer some basic principles as a starting point in drafting a blueprint for workplace democracy."[17]

These might be considered strange words coming from a business consultant, but they express very well the viewpoint of someone who puts business considerations second to political values. To the author of these words and to others at the Industrial Cooperatives Association (ICA) in Somerville, Mas-

---

[16]Ibid.

[17]David Ellerman, "ESOPs, Second Class Ownership," *Workplace Democracy,* Winter 1983, p. 18.

sachusetts, worker ownership is essentially about democracy. Accordingly, the ICA's role is to help workers form businesses in which democratic values are preserved. These business take the form of cooperatives; as such, they qualify for special tax benefits.

But as far as the ICA is concerned, tax benefits and higher productivity are not the point; democracy is. A primary rule in these co-ops is that voting rights are allocated on the basis of the one-person, one-vote principle. Also, because the ICA's co-op is conceived of as a democratic entity rather than as a business organization, there is essentially no such thing as "owning" a part of it; accordingly, at no time can a worker think of selling his or her share in the co-op. When you retire, you receive only the accumulated income that might have been credited to your account; no ownership rights go with you.

This severing of any relation between co-op shares and the marketplace introduces a potentially serious flaw in the ICA model; it removes a vital financial incentive for the co-op to plan for the long term. The stock market is interested only in the future; what someone is willing to pay you for your shares of stock is based on that person's assessment of the company's future performance. It is this market discipline that motivates long-term planning. Certain kinds of long-term planning may sacrifice a company's short-term profitability. But the price of the company's shares will still rise if the stock market perceives that the company has substantially enhanced its long-term prospects.

Now imagine a co-op in which the majority of workers are close to retirement. Since their only chance at financial gain can occur while they work for the co-op, they'll have a financial incentive to maximize short-term profitability to the possible detriment of the long term. On the other hand, if there were a market for their shares, there would be no such bias.

This issue aside, there is no question that the ICA has introduced a powerful concept into the debate over gainsharing. It is a concept that harkens back directly to the "industrial homesteading" that Ronald Reagan spoke of in the quote with which this chapter began.

Taming Inflation

I wonder why there has been so much apparent resistance, by labor and management, to planned arrangements for sharing in prosperity or adversity, in the latter instance in ways other than lay-offs alone. I am thinking, of course, of profit sharing plans or other ways of rewarding workers when things are good, without building in a floor on costs that may turn out to be unbearable.[18]

The speaker is Paul Volcker, chairman of the Federal Reserve.

Mr. Volcker was pointing to the potential for profit-sharing and similar gainsharing plans to check inflation while minimizing layoffs. If wage increases depend on profitability, then wages will go up only if profits do also. And if that happens, then wages will no longer push up prices. In an interview he granted in 1958, the late Walter Reuther made this very point. According to Reuther:

What we ought to do is to work out the equities in two stages in which we deliberately understate the size of the equity of the wage earner in our minimum demand, so that we will be certain it will have no inflationary impact. . . . Give us a down payment now—represented by our minimum demand—and we will defer the realization of the balance of our equity until you've completed the year, the consumer has paid his price, and you've made your profits.[19]

Under this arrangement, unemployment will also be minimized. Since profit sharing means that wages go down as well as up, it also means that labor costs can automatically decline in bad times. For instance, assume Reuther's down-payment approach. In a profitable year, labor gets its minimum demand plus a share of the profits; in an unprofitable year the mini-

---

[18]Paul Volcker, remarks at the dedication of the John Gray Institute of Lamar University, Beaumont, Texas, November 11, 1983, p. 14.

[19]"How Do We Live with Bigness? Interview," *The New Republic*, July 21, 1982, p. 15.

mum demand becomes the wage. If that happens, cost pressures would ease and layoffs could be substantially reduced.

Viewed from this perspective, even if such gainsharing plans had no positive effect on productivity, they could have an enormous positive effect on employment and therefore on overall output. In particular, say that the government is imposing monetary restraint on the economy in order to put a brake on inflation. A tragic side effect of tight money is unemployment. But with gainsharing general throughout the economy, then prices and wages would be downwardly flexible. The result would be that unemployment would be substantially diminished; and with higher employment, the economy's output would be higher as well.[20]

Conclusion

We have now completed our guided tour up the inverted pyramid of gainsharing. It should be clear by now that the case for gainsharing draws on our belief in the efficacy of the market system. If we had to explain why economies based on this system enjoy the highest productivity the world has ever seen, we would give one principal reason: The market recognizes that financial incentives are a prime motivator of work behavior. The advocates of gainsharing seek to give the fullest possible scope to this idea by making financial incentives a part of everyone's working life.

---

[20]For more on this, see Daniel J. B. Mitchell, "Gain-Sharing: An Anti-inflation Reform," *Challenge*, July/August 1982. Professor Mitchell proposes tax incentives to support gainsharing approaches of this kind.

Section 2

A Tale of Two Countries: What the United States Can Learn from Japan

Chapter 6

The Effects of Discrimination: Some Things We Shouldn't Learn

A New Faith

Is there anything we can learn from Japan about people and productivity?

The past few years have produced enough print about that question to fill a library. Conferences and college courses on Japanese management amount to a minor industry. There are even indications that our interest in the subject is degenerating into a new faith. For instance, consider the extraordinary popularity of a paperback entitled *The Book of Five Rings: The Real Art of Japanese Management.* Instead of living up to

---

[1]Miyamoto Musashi, *The Book of Five Rings: The Real Art of Japanese Management* (New York: Bantam Books, 1982).

its subtitle, the book turns out to be a text on fighting by a Japanese samurai warrior who lived in the 17th century. Some of its sections bear the following titles, all of them meant literally: "To Stab at the Face," "To Stab the Heart," "The 'Slapping Away' Parry," and "The Order of Opponents When Fighting Alone."[2] At a conference on Japanese management held in New York City, a professor from a prestigious business school read passages from this book to an audience of corporate managers. One passage he read was as follows: "When you want to see, see right at once. When you begin to think, you miss the point."[3] The sorry spectacle of a business school professor telling American managers not to think can only make one wonder whether America's fascination with Japan will become yet another reason for the decline in our productivity growth.[4]

It may be partly a response to these excesses that a backlash has set in. A host of critics are now beginning to tell us, partly with good reason, that not all is so well with Japan's way of doing things.[5] The viewpoint we will defend here is that much *can* be learned from Japan regarding people and productivity. But let us first acknowledge those aspects of the Japanese example that Americans had best leave unlearned.

Discrimination and Productivity

Item: By American standards, Japanese society practices discrimination against women. For instance, although women can rise in the professions, it is difficult for them to get high

---

[2]Ibid., pp. 47–50.

[3]Ibid., p. xxii.

[4]Witnessed by a New York Stock Exchange economist who attended this conference.

[5]See, for example, B. Bruce Briggs, "The Dangerous Folly Called Theory Z," *Fortune,* May 17, 1982.

paying managerial jobs with corporations. On the nonmanagerial level, companies that offer lifetime employment usually offer it only to men; women who are accorded this status must agree never to leave for marriage or motherhood. In general, then, companies view women as temporary help and will lay them off in bad times. The inferior status of women workers helps create a pattern frequently observed by visitors to Japan: In service industries, three women may be employed at a job that one could perform. Since women's promotional opportunities are extremely limited, they can be paid relatively little. And because of these low wages, a business can employ a surplus of female labor at relatively low cost. In a nondiscriminatory work environment, this inefficient use of labor probably would prove too costly.[6]

Item: Japan has a Korean minority numbering almost one half of one percent of the total population. They are mostly second and third generation and are assimilated in language and education. But they are largely denied citizenship and are shut out of most good job opportunities.[7]

Item: The Japanese economy offers young people virtually no "second chance." A young person who does badly in high school will be permanently barred from high-level jobs. His fate is sealed because access to good jobs comes only from attending a good university—which in turn comes only from doing well on entrance exams. So the indiscretions of youth can be the handicap of a lifetime.[8]

Item: "Core" companies—the Japanese counterpart of the Fortune 500—do not permit lateral job hopping. If you are unhappy working for Company A, there is no chance of getting a job with Company B. Unhappy or not, you are stuck for

---

[6]For further discussion, see "The Status of Women in Japanese Society," Appendix 1 of this book, p. 149.

[7]See Richard H. Mitchell, *The Korean Minority in Japan* (Berkeley: University of California Press, 1967).

[8]Thomas P. Rohlen, "Japanese Education and Society," unpublished manuscript, 1982, p. 23. Rohler, an anthropologist, is an expert's expert on Japan.

life—unless you are willing to take a job with a company on the periphery.[9]

Item: The core companies impose mandatory retirement on nonmanagerial workers who are 55 to 60 years old, even though most of them are quite able to continue working. What many of these people do in order to support themselves is get lower-paying jobs with companies on the periphery.[10]

All of these items are forms of discrimination. Some of them violate our sense of fair play, others our sense of justice. And in fact, most of them would violate our laws.[11] But what also can be said about them is that they detract from overall productivity. When employers practice discrimination, they deny themselves and society full access to the productive potential of the work force. Talented women, talented Koreans, talented people whose only drawback is that they performed poorly in high school, all are being underutilized in relation to their talents. A similar point applies to people over 55 who could remain productive at their jobs if they were allowed to retain them and to people who could be more productive at another company if they were allowed to move.

To say the least, Americans have no cause for self-righteousness when it comes to another country's discriminatory practices. But what does appear to distinguish us from Japan is our greater public awareness that these evils exist and our very real efforts to reform them. In that regard, the Japanese may have something to learn from us.

The Japanese College: A Four-Year Vacation

Another lesson to leave unlearned from the Japanese applies to their system of higher education. In the next chapter, we

---

[9]Ibid., pp. 17–18, plus interviews with Dr. Rohlen. This rigidity also has its positive side; see Chapter 3.

[10]Based on interviews with Dr. Thomas P. Rohlen. For further discussion, see "The Economics of Japan's Seniority System," Appendix 1, p. 149.

[11]We are indebted to Isaac Shapiro, a partner in the New York-based law firm of Milbank, Tweed, Hadley & McCloy, for making this point.

will be taking note of the extraordinary effectiveness of their primary and secondary schools, but their colleges are another matter altogether. Over 40 percent of high school graduates attend some kind of college.[12] For the vast majority of them, the first two years amount to an extended vacation; for most of those who are planning on business as a career, the vacation lasts all four years. On being asked by a New York Stock Exchange interviewer whether his college experience had been demanding, a young Japanese economist who had attended an elite university flashed a grin and described it as a "paradise." He added that he had not heard of anybody ever being expelled from college for academic reasons; students were expelled only for being in trouble with the police.[13]

From an American perspective, there is something ironic about the school experience of a young Japanese man planning on a managerial career in business. After putting up an extraordinary effort to distinguish himself in primary and secondary school, he wins acceptance to a good university. Nothing further is expected of him until he applies for a corporate job. Graduating from an elite college is all he needs in order to be considered for a position with a good company; his academic performance while attending that college matters not at all. Since companies do not expect their applicants to have degrees beyond undergraduate school, recruiting happens in a young man's senior year.

While some might theorize that this four-year interregnum is a good way to provide young people with an opportunity to unwind from the responsibilities behind them and the responsibilities to come, the rest of us might wonder why the process has to go on for so long. Companies actually know full well that most of their college-educated entrants have grown soft from four years of easy living; the training program they put them through once they are hired is partly aimed at toughening them up. While it is unlikely that young people

---

[12]Rohlen, "Japanese Education," p. 8.

[13]Based on an interview with Japanese economist Yoshiaki Taguchi, March 18, 1982.

are harmed in any long-lasting way by their college experience, there still must be better ways for them to spend their time.[14]

But if Japanese society is flawed in ways that detract from its productivity, there are also many things that it does right. Indeed, the things that it does right have to be all that much more effective in order to compensate for what it does wrong. The next three chapters will deal with those things that we *can* learn from Japan about people and productivity.

---

[14]Based on interviews with Dr. Thomas P. Rohlen. See also Edwin O. Reischauer, *The Japanese* (Cambridge, Mass.: Harvard University Press, 1977). Reischauer writes: "That Japan continues to operate as well as it does despite the problems of higher education seems at first surprising but probably is explained by the excellence of preuniversity education and the system of advanced in-service training for new employees in business and government" (p. 178).

"Education is the cheap defense of nations."

Edmund Burke

Chapter 7

Preparing People for Work I: Schooling

What happens in the workplace is significantly determined by the preparation and training for work that people receive before they get to the workplace. Among the lessons we can learn from Japan about people and productivity, this relatively neglected area may be the most important. But since we also must understand how these lessons can be applied, this chapter and the next will say as much about the United States as they do about Japan.

The Importance of Schooling in Japan

We recently put the following question to an expert on Japan: "If you had to pick the one factor that is responsible for the extraordinarily high productivity of the Japanese people, what would that factor be?" He answered unhesitatingly: the high quality of Japanese primary and secondary education.[1]

---

[1]Based on an interview with Isaac Shapiro, a New York lawyer who was born in Tokyo in 1931 and grew up in Japan through the war years and the first year of the American occupation. He has written extensively about his native country and was, for a number of years, president of the Japan Society in New York.

Education? Not quality circles, the art of Japanese management, the practice of "Theory Z," or the partnership between government and business? No, he insisted, whatever
those factors may contribute, the key factor is the schools. He
pointed out that a similar view is held by no less an authority
than Harvard University Professor Edwin O. Reischauer, former ambassador to Japan and author of numerous books about
that country. Reischauer writes in his most recent book, *The
Japanese,* that "nothing, in fact, is more central in Japanese
society or more basic to Japan's success than is its educational
system."[2]

Whether it is correct to say that the Japanese schools are
the key to their productivity performance, few can doubt that
the schools play an important role. For instance, consider the
fact that during Japan's postwar economic miracle, there was
a concomitant revolution going on in the schooling of its people. After the war, the Japanese government vigorously pur-
sued the goal of a universal high school education.[3] In 1950,
43 percent of all 15-year-olds were going on to high school;
this figure increased steadily until it surpassed 90 percent by
1975 and 95 percent by 1980. Over the same period, among
younger age groups, enrollment in nursery school and kinder-
garten increased from a small minority to the overwhelming
majority of all four- and five-year-olds. The addition of the
first two years of schooling is significant, since it is there that
Japanese children learn how to read. Japanese born from 1910
to 1945 tested at an average IQ of 102–105, while subsequent
tests showed an average of 108–115 among Japanese born

---

[2]Edwin O. Reischauer, *The Japanese* (Cambridge, Mass.: Harvard University
Press, 1977), p. 167.

[3]This material on the Japanese school system is drawn from Thomas P. Rohlen, *Japan's High Schools* (Berkeley: University of California Press, 1983); Thomas
P. Rohlen, "Japanese Education and Society," unpublished manuscript, 1982; Ronald S. Anderson, *Education in Japan: A Century of Modern Development* (Washington, D.C.: U.S. Government Printing Office, 1975); and William K. Cummings,
Education and Equality in Japan (Princeton, N.J.: Princeton University Press,
1980). Also drawn from interviews with Dr. Rohlen.

from 1946 to 1969.[4] At least some of this significant increase in mental ability must be attributable to the increase in the general level of education—and that, in turn, must partially explain the extraordinary growth in productivity over this same period.

Intercountry comparisons provide further evidence of the connection between education and productivity in Japan: With one of the highest rates of productivity growth in the world, the Japanese people are among the best educated. For instance, compare Japan with the United States, where productivity growth has been much lower. Approximately 95 percent of Japanese teenagers now graduate from high school compared with approximately 74 percent in the United States.[5] Japan's schools are in session five and a half days a week, with more weeks to the school year than U.S. schools. The result is that a graduate of a Japanese high school has the equivalent of approximately four more full years of schooling than a U.S. high school graduate. International surveys of educational achievement show that in both math and science, the mean scores of schoolchildren in Japan are higher than in any other country, and far higher than in the United States. Also, among Japanese the degree of variability around the mean is one of the lowest—which testifies to the fact that educational achievement in Japan is widespread.[6]

The success of the Japanese school system in reaching the broad masses of people is a recurrent theme among students of the subject. For instance, in his study of Japanese high schools, Dr. Thomas P. Rohlen writes:

> The great accomplishment of Japanese primary and secondary education lies not in its creation of a brilliant elite, . . . but in

---

[4]Richard Lynn, "IQ in Japan and the United States Shows a Growing Disparity," *Nature*, May 20, 1982, pp. 222–23. For additional discussion, see "IQ and Education in Japan," Appendix 1, p. 150.

[5]U.S. figure from a telephone interview on October 14, 1982, with Paul Houts of the Carnegie Foundation for the Advancement of Teaching.

[6]For data, see "Math and Science Mean Scores," Appendix 1, p. 151.

its generation of such a high *average* level of capability. The profoundly impressive fact is that it is shaping a whole population, workers as well as managers, to a standard inconceivable in the United States, where we are still trying to implement high school graduate competency tests that measure only minimal reading and computing skills.[7]

U.S. Schools

As Dr. Rohlen implies, to discuss the performance of the U.S. and Japanese school systems in the same context is like attempting to compare two unlike objects. In the United States, the role of the schools in affecting productivity may loom even larger than in Japan—but more as a brake than as an accelerator. The regretable fact is that many of our people are poorly prepared even for the minimal requirements of the workplace.

To appreciate the magnitude of the problem, consider the recent findings of the National Assessment of Educational Progress, which surveyed the knowledge and skills of high school students. The survey showed that: 13 percent could not perform reading tasks designated as "functional"; 28 percent could not answer questions testing "literal comprehension" of what they read; almost 10 percent could not write prose deemed marginally acceptable. The results were much worse with regard to anything beyond basic skills. For instance, 53 percent could not write a letter correcting a billing error, and 43 percent could not handle even the simplest problems involving applied math. Bear in mind that these results were restricted to high school students. Had the survey included the approximately 26 percent of young people who

---

[7]Rohlen, *Japan's High Schools*, p. 322. The success of the Japanese school system in reaching the broad masses of people is the main thesis in Cummins, *Education and Equality*.

drop out of school, then the proportion of those performing poorly would undoubtedly have been much higher.[8]

In case there is a doubt about the validity of these findings, consider the results of the recent adult performance level study, conducted by the University of Texas. Based on a representative sample of the U.S. population, the study found that approximately one in five adults is unable to handle such tasks as completing an employment application, balancing a checkbook, interpreting a calorie chart, properly addressing an envelope, and applying for a loan. On that basis the study concludes that one fifth of U.S. adults are "functionally incompetent."[9]

The Need for Action

The Japanese example reminds us that a productive society requires an educated work force. It also reminds us of some of the things needed to restore the effectiveness of our schools: a return to basics, persistent standards applied to the teaching of those basics, and a strong community consensus supporting those standards. Some have blamed the shortcomings of our schools on the supposed shortcomings of our young people. If that viewpoint is valid, then we must conclude that nothing can be done until our young people change. To those who persist in this belief, we recommend the words of the noted psychologist and social critic Dr. Kenneth Clark:

> I went to school in Harlem and I remember my teachers in Junior High School 139. I knew Miss McGuire insisted that I

---

[8]Based on a May 12, 1982, telephone interview with a researcher from the National Assessment for Educational Progress, Denver, Colorado. For a full discussion, see Charles J. Gadway, *Functional Literacy: Basic Reading Performance* (Washington, D.C.: National Right to Read Effort, 1976); and Roy H. Forbes and Lynn Grover Gisi, *Information Society: Will Our High School Graduates Be Ready?* (Denver, Colo.: Education Commission of the States, March 1982).

[9]Adult Performance Level Project, *Final Report: The Adult Performance Level Study* (Austin: University of Texas, March 1975).

respect the structure of a sentence and she explained to me what a sentence was. Those teachers had standards that we knew we had to meet. Why is it that that could be done in the late 1920s and the early 1930s and not in the 1970s and 1980s. Why?

All of them—Mr. Deegan, Miss McGuire, Miss Smith, and Mr. Mitchell—never asked whether I came from a broken home. They weren't social workers; they were teachers.[10]

In effect, Dr. Clark is telling us there is no excuse for inaction.

All that must be done to reform the schools—and what further we might learn from the example of others, including the Japanese—is a subject that is well beyond the scope of this study. What we want to focus on here is one relatively neglected aspect of this issue: the role that businesspeople could play.

What Business Can Do

Even in more normal times, there is a strong case to be made for a deepened business involvement in our schools. If the first purpose of our schools is to create good citizens, the second is to create productive people. Business ought to do all it reasonably can to help our schools fulfill that second purpose, even if productivity growth were soaring and our classrooms were models of effectiveness. Indeed, the more effective our schools become, the more they can benefit from business involvement—and the more the schools can contribute to a productive and prosperous work force.

Given the circumstances we face now, the need for business involvement in our schools has become particularly acute. And in fact, some measures are being taken already. More than new ideas, we need stepped-up business involve-

---

[10]Quoted in Gene I. Maeroff, *Don't Blame the Kids: The Trouble with America's Public Schools* (New York: McGraw-Hill, 1982). p. 83.

ment in those approaches that already have proven to be viable. Here are some of the possibilities.

More businesses might get involved in "adopt a school" programs. Say that a corporation decides to adopt a school in its local area. Such a relationship would involve responding to the school's particular needs. Does the school have many students whose math skills are poor and who could benefit from one-to-one tutoring? Staff of the corporation could get training in math tutoring and provide it to those students who need it. Are there special curriculum materials required for students who have reading problems? The corporation might provide the funds to purchase those materials. Would the school benefit from offering a course in word processing or from the use of computers as teaching devices? The corporation might provide the school with the use of that equipment.

What incentives would a corporation have to become so involved with a school? We can think of several. To begin with, the involvement could be a part of a company's recruitment process: Students who are helped by the company might eventually become its employees. In that way, the company would get the direct benefit of a better skilled labor force. Second, there is the favorable publicity that results from being associated with activities of this sort. And finally, there is the boost to staff morale that results from such deep involvement in the activities of the community, particularly if staff of the company have children attending the school that is receiving this support. In fact, adopting a school is nothing new. In Los Angeles, for example, there is an adopt-a-school program with 105 businesses currently participating. As part of the program, the Los Angeles office of the Prudential Insurance Company sends 50 of its employees to a local elementary school to tutor students once a week.[11] More companies and more localities should be involved in such activities.

More businesses might open their doors to work-study

[11]Based on a telephone interview in August 1982 with Ted Falk of the Prudential Insurance Company of America, Western Home Office.

programs with nearby high schools and colleges. Young people who want to be auto mechanics, word processors, computer programmers, retail buyers, and office managers could spend a good part of their school time learning these trades on the job. What we are talking about, in other words, is a revival of the apprenticeship system, which was based on the sound premise that many tasks are better learned on the job. The agreement between master and apprentice was one of mutual benefit: The apprentice received training, and the master received the services of an assistant. In this case, businesses and schools could work out similar arrangements. Such programs could go a long way toward boosting the functional competence of young people.

Business could be directly involved with curriculum development of career education programs, from the elementary school to the college level. Businesspeople could work with curriculum planners to clarify the skills required in the whole range of jobs available in the business sector. Career-education programs also could include businesspeople visiting classrooms and students visiting businesses. Then career training could play a more important role in aiding intelligent career choices.

Businesspeople could meet regularly with educators to provide ideas and information that could increase the effectiveness of the schools. For instance, what will be the needs of the job market in the next decade? What is it about the education of young employees that could be strengthened? What kinds of adult education programs might the school develop that could supplement the skills of older workers?

If these and other ideas are to have a chance of being adopted, there must first be an effort to raise business's awareness about their stake in the problems the school face. We must understand that schooling is a long-term investment in human capital, and that productivity suffers when that investment is neglected. The disturbing fact is that even if we were to reverse that neglect tomorrow, we may spend years before we overcome its legacy. The time to begin is now.

"The larger a company becomes, the faster it gets taken over by the accountants, the lawyers, and the bottom-liners who live in a world of reports, charts, graphs, projections, and chalk talks."

William Attwood, former president of Newsday

Chapter 8

Preparing People for Work II: Training Managers[1]

Japan's way of schooling its people resembles our own in many respects; but their way of training their corporate managers is almost completely different. In fact, even if their way were far better, we would not be able to adopt it completely. But some elements of what the Japanese do are worth considering.

Front-Lines Experience

Imagine General Motors hiring M.B.A.s from elite schools and then requiring that they spend their first year working on the assembly line. Preposterous? Maybe—but something almost exactly like it is the custom at one of GM's chief competitors, Honda Motors of Japan. Honda requires a full year of factory work from its newly hired university graduates. The man-

---

[1]Most of the information in this chapter is based on interviews with Dr. Thomas P. Rohlen.

agers-to-be are dispersed throughout the factory floor and re-port to the first-level supervisors. In that way, their first ex-perience of the company is no different from that of any other entry-level person's. Nor is Honda unique in this practice. In one way or another most large Japanese companies require a kind of front lines experience from their managers-in-training.

The main purpose of front-lines experience is to help in-still in the manager an understanding both of the basic processes of his company and of the people who are an insep-arable part of those processes. The nature of the experience a newcomer gets depends on how his company defines the front lines. Banks often require that people put in time as tellers. Matsushita Electric Company, which has retail stores all over Japan selling its products, requires that its incoming college graduates work in these stores as salesmen for several months. One extreme example is a well-known furniture manufacturer that requires managers to spend three years calling on purchasing departments of prospective customers. There are graduates from elite universities who fail miserably in this endeavor: Good at their studies, they turn out to be not so good at making cold calls. But even if they are destined to work in the company's accounting department—where poor salesmanship is presumably no great drawback—they are not let off the hook. They are told that they must spend more time in sales until they find the personal capacity to do it right. Since there is nowhere else to go—you don't switch companies in Japan—they have no choice but to keep trying.

Belief in the benefits of front-lines experience extends to the government as well. For instance, Japan's Ministry of Ag-riculture and Fishery imposes a special requirement on train-ees who have passed the qualifying exams to become ranking officials. The young officials-to-be must spend one month in the hinterland living with and working for a farmer or fisherman.[2]

---

[2]Based on correspondence from Japanese economist Yoshiaki Taguchi, July 26, 1982.

A Long Apprenticeship

Front-lines experience must be viewed in the context of the whole approach the Japanese company takes to training its managers. The Japanese company generally hires young men right out of college who have had little or no classroom training that directly prepares them for their vocation. In the company's view, they have had little that equips them to work cooperatively with people. The route that leads from high school to business generally looks like this: First, a high school senior must do well enough on difficult college entrance exams to gain admission to a prestigious university. Then follow four years of college during which he may never take a business-related course and where very little is expected of him in any case. In his senior year he takes written aptitude tests given by the well-established companies that he would like to work for. These tests are rudimentary and are given only to eliminate the more inadequate candidates; no one who was able to score high on the much tougher university entrance exams could fail to do well on them. After passing these tests, he is granted job interviews. Since a company will be making a decision to employ an applicant for life, the personality he projects at these interviews is the primary determinant of whether he will be hired.

Once an applicant gets a job, his real training begins. Whatever he may have lost from four undemanding years in college, he very quickly regains. To begin with, the company fills the role of business school—in most cases by providing on-the-job training, but often through the literal equivalent of school. For instance, Dr. Thomas Rohlen writes of the "Uedagin" bank that maintains a separate training institute with seven full-time staff members; one third of the personnel of the bank receive some training at the institute every year.[3] To

---

[3]Thomas P. Rohlen, *For Harmony and Strength: Japanese White-Collar Organization in Anthropological Perspective* (Berkeley: University of California Press, 1974), p. 194. "Uedagin" is the pseudonym of a bank that is approximately the 30th largest in Japan. Dr. Rohlen worked there as a participant-observer for a year during 1968–69. *For Harmony and Strength* is based on that experience.

take another example, Sony is well known for being a university unto itself, with extensive programs in languages, finance, science, and engineering.

But in addition to technical training, Japanese companies also emphasize training in the intangible: in knowledge of oneself, knowledge of one's organization, and in the skills required to work with other people. Front-lines experience is an important part of this training; in addition, many companies require a kind of "boot camp" experience as well. This generally consists of a period of several weeks in which young recruits are brought together to experience group living, formal instruction, and a series of unique ordeals aimed at building their character. In his book on the Uedagin bank, Dr. Rohlen vividly describes what the bank's boot camp is like. On the first day the young men are told the following: "In the public schools, all you had to do was study for examinations. Whether you got along with your fellow classmates or not was not very important. Here, we have cooperative living as our style of life."[4] The ordeals the young men are put through include an endurance walk of 25 miles and a unique experience called *roto* (a word for which the best translation is "bewilderment"). In this case, each individual trainee has to go from house to house in a nearby town and offer to work without pay; he is to do whatever his host asks of him and is forbidden to explain who he is or why he is there. Dr. Rohlen draws the following conclusions about this experience:

> In the course of begging for work, that is, begging for acceptance by others, the subject learns of the superficial nature of much in his daily life. It is expected that his reliance on affiliations, titles, ranks and a circle of those close to him will be revealed, and, perhaps for the first time, he will begin to ask who he really is. Roto also provides a unique opportunity for a trusting and compassionate interaction between strangers. After a roto experience, it is unlikely that the person will continue to disregard

---

[4]Ibid., p. 201.

the humanity of others, no matter how strange they are to him in terms of social relationship.[5]

Training in the intangible continues well beyond this early period. In the Japanese company, there is no such thing as the fast track. A young man will generally spend years in a series of relatively low-level jobs before he can begin to assume managerial responsibility. This teaches him technical skills, but it also provides him with a deeply felt knowledge of the people of his organization.

In a previous chapter, we faulted the Japanese system for preventing people from switching employers. Here we should note what some perceive to be an important benefit arising from that rigidity: Companies find it cost effective to make enormous investments in training their managers, since they can plan on reaping the full payoff from their investment.

Applicability

In the United States, the system is very different. No graduate of an elite business school would spend a year working on any company's factory floor, even for the starting salary that such graduates are used to getting; and few American companies could afford to take the other side of the bargain. Few companies are likely to spend years preparing people for managerial responsibility only to find that some executive recruiter woos them away to a competitor. Compared with the Japanese, our managers get far more business training in the classrooms— and less of it on the job. In general, they serve a much shorter apprenticeship before assuming executive positions. They may be better trained in corporate strategy than their Japanese counterparts, but it is probably fair to say that they are not so well trained in the human knowledge of the organizations they run.

---

[5]Ibid., pp. 204–5.

Does this put American companies at a disadvantage? There is no way to prove that it does. And in any case, it would not be cost effective for most American companies to fully replicate the Japanese approach.

Nonetheless, any company that wants to rethink its policies in this area might consider the Japanese example. There are always trade-offs in deciding what people to hire, what people to promote, and what attributes to encourage among managers. A company that required some front-lines experience from its M.B.A.s might find that some of those from elite schools are declining to apply; if it required a longer apprenticeship from its managers-in-training, it might find that some are quitting in disgust before the apprenticeship is through. But it might also find that through such policies, it is creating a core of managers who have a marrow-deep knowledge of the organization and how it works and that the benefits of this achievement exceed the costs.

"I'll hate to see him go back to Japan. He always thanks you for anything extra you do. He's probably the best boss I've ever had."

statement of an American worker about his supervisor in a Japanese-owned plant, 1982

Chapter 9

East Meets West: Japanese-Owned Businesses in the United States

---

So far in this discussion of Japan, we have focused on the Japanese way of preparing people for the workplace. Now we turn to the issue that has gotten by far the most attention in this country: the practices of Japanese management.

In this case, we take a novel approach. When the best-selling book *The Art of Japanese Management* was reviewed in *The New York Times*, the reviewer commented that "it would not be easy for Americans to adopt the Japanese model, much of which arises out of its country's culture."[1] Accordingly, we have commissioned one of the coauthors of that book, Stanford Business School Professor Richard Tanner Pas-

---

[1] *The New York Times Book Review*, February 28, 1982, p. 35.

cale, to address that issue.[2] Professor Pascale closely examined a group of companies whose top management is Japanese and whose work force is American: U.S.-based subsidiaries of Japanese corporations. In all the cases that Pascale looked at, the Japanese have chosen not to be absentee owners; rather, they have brought over their own nationals to run things according to their lights. How have these missionaries fared with the natives? The answer to that question should tell us a great deal about how easy or hard it is for Americans to adopt the Japanese model.

Findings

We can summarize Professor Pascale's conclusions as follows:

- A Japanese-run company with an American work force does indeed make for a corporate environment that is different in certain respects from an American-run company with an American work force. In other words, the Japanese management model *is* operating on American soil, even though it is unquestionably different from Japanese management on Japanese soil.
- The Japanese subsidiaries are not more productive than American companies in a strictly quantitative sense. However, the evidence shows that they pay more attention than American companies to product quality.

---

[2]This chapter is based primarily on "Japanese Management Practices in the United States," a background paper prepared especially for the New York Stock Exchange by Professor Pascale and Professor Mary Ann Maguire of Catholic University. The paper updated research into this subject done in the mid-1970s by Professors Pascale and Maguire. All quotes in this chapter are from that paper unless otherwise indicated. In the text of this chapter, we cite Pascale as sole analyst for the sake of brevity.

Method

Professor Pascale closely examined a sample of 13 Japanese firms in the United States. These firms represent 10 different industries that include a broad range of activities: banking, retailing, food processing, transportation, bearings, fasteners, motorcycle assembly, electronics, aircraft manufacture, and automotive distribution. The choice therefore included both the service sector and the manufacturing sector as well as industries with both low and high technological content. In general, the parent companies in Japan are high performers in their fields; otherwise, they would be in no position to absorb the risk and expense of opening up American subsidiaries. All of these subsidiaries were headed by a Japanese national; all had Japanese nationals in two or three key positions, and on the average, Japanese nationals represented about a quarter of those employed in management, with these heavily concentrated in staff positions. On the other hand, the work force was American, as were the overwhelming majority of line managers.

Pascale compared these 13 Japanese companies with American companies that were similar in major respects. In each case, he carefully matched the Japanese subsidiary with an American counterpart. The matching criteria included kind of product, type of technology, size and composition of work force, and geographical location. In Pascale's sample, some of the companies matched with their American counterparts were: Sony and Zenith, Japan Airlines and United Airlines, Toyota auto distributors and Ford auto distributors, Shirokiya department stores and J. C. Penney, Kawasaki and Harley Davidson, Mitsubishi Aircraft and Aerocommander, YKK and Talon.

To ensure confidentiality to the study participants, our discussion will include few references to particular companies. Rather, it will report general conclusions about Japanese-run companies versus those that are American-run. Note that the statements to follow will not apply to *all* Japanese-run companies or *all* American-run companies, but rather will apply to them on balance.

A Better Place to Work

With the help of survey questionnaires as well as open-ended interviews, Pascale found a number of differences in management style between the Japanese-owned companies and their American counterparts. The differences add up to one overall impression: An American who knew these facts would probably choose to work for a Japanese-managed firm rather than a firm managed by other Americans.

Consulting with subordinates. Pascale found that slightly more middle-level managers in the Japanese firms reported that their immediate superior consulted with them on non-routine decisions (76 percent in the Japanese case versus 71 percent in the American case). But what is significant is the nature of the consultations. The respondents were asked to distinguish between being asked for "factual input" versus being asked for "their opinions and recommendations."

> Of the two options [Pascale writes], managers in *American* firms were more likely to describe their superiors as getting only factual information from subordinates; managers in Japanese firms were more likely to say that their superiors consult with subordinates for opinions and recommendations. This subtlety of consulting more fully with subordinates is probably the most significant distinction between Japanese and American decision making.[3]

Job security. The findings also showed that the Japanese firms placed greater emphasis on job security than did the American firms. None of these firms offered the lifetime em-

---

[3]For data, see "Comparative Patterns of Decision Making in Japanese- and American-Managed Firms," Appendix 1, Table A–5, p. 153.

ployment that is available at the parent company in Japan, but the record shows serious and largely effective efforts to avoid layoffs. During the recession of 1974–75 only one of the Japanese-owned firms had laid off any employees, whereas seven of the American companies had done so. In terms of number of employees, this meant that the Japanese laid off 2.8 percent of their work force during the early period, compared with 11.8 percent for American companies. Pascale has no data for the American companies during the 1982 slowdown; but for the Japanese companies, his data again show that only one of the Japanese companies had laid anyone off.

Top managers in the Japanese-owned firms stressed the importance of job security. In a recent interview, the president and chief operating officer of Sony said about its American subsidiary that "we have not absolutely committed ourselves and said, 'we will never lay you off,' but we have communicated it psychologically."[4] Other Japanese firms recognize a similar commitment. For instance, a representative of one firm stated that "as a practical matter, it is difficult to lay employees off" because to do so "would destroy the positive image Japanese firms have created up to now."[5]

Similarly, an executive of YKK has said, "We don't promise, but we announce we will endeavor not to lay employees off." He added, "If we face difficulty, we first proportionately reduce the wages of all employees from general manager down to lowest-paid employee, other than probationary workers. Only if we can't manage do we resort to a layoff."[6]

Pascale notes two other strategies Japanese companies use to avoid layoffs. One is job rotation—the shifting of workers from one job to another, a practice that helps create a work force able to perform a variety of jobs. In the event of a cutback, the company may be able to reassign workers to vacancies in other parts of the company, rather than lay these

---

[4]"How the Japanese Managed in the U.S.," *Fortune,* June 15, 1981, p. 98.

[5]Japanese External Trade Organization, "Japanese Manufacturing Operations in the United States" (New York: JETRO, 1981), p. 45.

[6]"How the Japanese Managed," p. 102.

workers off. A second strategy is used in conjunction with job rotation: the practice of filling vacancies with temporary workers when a slowdown appears likely. If the slowdown occurs, the temporary workers are discharged and replaced by regular workers, who are shifted from other operations within the company.

Firing for cause. Another related point is that there was a lower rate of firings among the Japanese firms (a mean of 11.3 percent of the work force for the Japanese firms over a one-year period versus a mean of 17.5 percent for the American firms). The explanation for this difference may lie in the way the companies dealt with absenteeism. To a far greater extent than the American firms, the Japanese companies dealt with the problem by fact-finding and counseling rather than by imposing penalties.[7] This different pattern indicates a greater willingness in the Japanese case to try to solve employee relations problems rather than allow situations to deteriorate until workers are fired.

Manager-worker relations. More often than in the American firms, managers in the Japanese firms were directly involved in the productive process. Pascale notes that:

- "Japanese managers would . . . frequently pitch in to help get the job done."
- "Middle and especially top-level managers . . . were more often found on the shop floor observing and/or conversing with line workers about their operations, machines, etc."
- "Japanese firms are . . . more likely to have 'open door' policies, where managers are accessible to employees at all levels of the hierarchy."

Pascale also notes that the Japanese firms spent almost three times as much as the American firms on company-

---

[7]For data, see "Comparative Ways of Dealing with Absenteeism in Japanese- and American-Managed Firms," Appendix 1, Table A–6, p. 153.

sponsored social and recreational activities: "The Japanese view these parties, picnics, teams, and tournaments as opportunities to improve communication, dissolve the working frictions of organizational life, and build trust."

Pascale also asked about levels of job satisfaction. Not surprisingly, he found that nonmanagers generally showed more satisfaction with their jobs at the Japanese firms than at the American firms. More often at the Japanese firms, they mentioned that the "company cared." As Pascale notes, "American employees in these firms refer positively to their working conditions, specifically noting job security and the concern of managers for their well-being and for the general state of affairs on the production floor."

Treatment of women. We began this review of Pascale's findings by saying that an American who knew these facts would probably prefer to work for a Japanese-managed company. But women who seek management positions may be an exception to that statement. In a previous chapter, we mentioned that in Japan it is difficult for women to get corporate jobs in management. Similarly, Pascale found in the mid-1970s that women in Japanese-managed firms more often expressed reservations about their possibilities for advancement to middle-management positions; and follow-up interviews he conducted in 1982 revealed very few women in middle management.[8]

Japanese Thoughts on American Workers

So far we have stressed what American workers thought of the Japanese. But what about the other way around? Here Pascale notes the following:

- Japanese managers "agreed that in comparison to Japanese workers, Americans wanted a more precise defini-

---

[8]Pascale's findings are comparatively mild. Two Japanese-owned companies not in his sample have been the targets of lawsuits by women employees charging discrimination.

tion of their job responsibilities and [that] . . . few would move beyond their respective job definitions." In this regard, Pascale points out that Japanese managers "prefer a less-strict definition of responsibility" while Americans "prefer the clearer delineation of responsibilities and accountability that job descriptions provide."

- "Very few Japanese firms have attempted to start quality circles in their U.S. operations. Managers in most Japanese firms indicate that employees first need more socialization (i.e., better teamwork)."[9]
- Japanese managers voiced no criticism about the willingness of American workers to do their assigned jobs, but several expressed dissatisfaction with their knowledge of mathematics—an important issue in high technology-industries.

An executive of YKK has said that one of his "most severe shocks" was seeing managers "in whom we had confidence" suddenly leaving to work for other companies. He added: "I don't know how lower-ranked employees can be motivated or imbued with a sense of company loyalty under such circumstances."[10]

Of course, anyone familiar with the difference between Japanese and American work cultures—or with our previous two chapters on preparation and training for work in Japan—would not be surprised by these observations. The Japanese are used to a more cohesive, more loyal, and better-educated work force than they have found in the United States.

Quantity and Quality

So far, with the exception of the treatment of women, we have drawn a positive picture of Japanese-managed firms in rela-

---

[9]For further discussion, see "Quality Circles among Japanese-Managed Companies in the United States," Appendix 1, p. 153.

[10]"How the Japanese Managed," p. 98.

tion to their U.S. counterparts. We do not want to exaggerate that picture. As we pointed out, Pascale compared Japanese-managed firms that were highly successful with American-managed firms that also were highly successful. Accordingly, Pascale found many similarities as well.

But the differences exist. And the question is, what effect, if any, do they have on actual company performance?

Pascale's findings were mixed. First, with regard to productivity as measured quantitatively, the results were a stand-off. In 5 of the 10 industries studied—1 service and 4 manufacturing—the Japanese companies were more productive. In the remaining five—two service and three manufacturing—the American companies were more productive. Pascale measured productivity as output per worker-hour by comparing similar operations performed in the Japanese and American companies.[11]

But with regard to product quality, Pascale's findings were quite different. He writes: "All firms, of course, need to attend to quality if they are to remain in business. What our observations and interviews lead us to conclude is that quality is assigned a higher priority in Japanese firms than in many, or perhaps most, American firms." In fact, Pascale found that in 6 of the 10 industries studied, the Japanese firms paid more attention to quality than did their American counterparts. Only in one case did the American-owned firm pay more attention to quality.

Several American managers noted that American firms for which they are or have been employed have been willing to accept higher reject rates to obtain higher volume production, while some Japanese companies are very concerned about reject rates of even one or two percent. As a manager at one Japanese firm explained: "If our production lines turn out two million pieces a day and even one percent are defective, if one quarter of

---

[11]For further discussion, see "Pascale's Methodology in Measuring Productivity," Appendix 1, p. 154.

these rejects are not caught, we are sending out into the market five thousand defective pieces *each day*. Whether a company turns out two million small, inexpensive items or twenty thousand more costly items, defects erode the reputation of the product and the company."

Pascale infers an inverse connection between attention to quality and the incidence of what he calls "counterproductive" behavior among employees. As one would expect, he found generally greater incidence of this behavior in the American firms. His findings were based on surveying non-managerial employees in both the American and Japanese firms about the incidence of such behavior among "people on your level of this organization":

> Five types of counterproductive behavior in American firms are of particular interest: (1) "not working as hard as possible," (2) "trying to get out of work," (3) "not letting on when short of work," (4) "just not caring about the job," and (5) "just not caring about the customer."

Attention to quality can, of course, have as much or more of an effect on a company's bottom line as attention to quantity.

Applicability to American-Owned Firms

What Japanese managers have brought to the United States is an attention to the nuances of decision making, to the job security of their employees, to worker well-being generally, and to product quality.

Pascale asked some of the American-owned firms why they did not pick up on the positive attributes of their Japanese competitors. In some areas, especially the preoccupation with quality production, he found that American firms are beginning to catch on. In other areas, American managers cited unions as an obstacle; they also pointed out that a much smaller proportion of Japanese-owned companies have to deal with unions.

For instance, unions are generally opposed to job rotation, even though it permits greater job security. Unions also have opposed allowing upper and middle management to be present on the production floor. This last practice is something that Japanese managers regard as central, both to keeping abreast of production difficulties and to maintaining good worker-management relations. It is noteworthy that one Japanese-owned company successfully negotiated with its employees' union a limited management presence on the shop floor. This case suggests that successful negotiations also may be possible regarding job rotation, once both parties accept job security as a goal.

In one sense, it is legitimate to speak of the factors we have mentioned as amounting to a style of management that is Japanese. But in another sense, the Japanese are simply reminding us of some of those attributes that make for good management—Japanese, American, or otherwise.

"People support that which they help create."

a survey respondent

Section 3

Human Resource Programs for Productivity: Findings of an NYSE Survey

"Punching in, catching hell, punching out. "

a workday in a steelmill[1]

Chapter 10

The Programs

What is American management currently doing to achieve more labor cooperation, to reduce costly adversarial tactics, to enhance the quality of production, and to raise the quality of work life? The New York Stock Exchange found many valuable case studies on this issue, but no comprehensive information. So we decided to fill this void.

Survey Scope

To profile corporations' efforts to develop their human resources, we surveyed a statistically representative sample of the approximately 49,000 U.S. corporations with 100 or more employees. These corporations employ about 41 million people and account for more than half of all private nonfarm employees.[2]

Our focus was broad: the entire array of human resource programs that contribute to improving worker performance.

---

[1]"Will the Slide Kill Quality Circles?" *Business Week*, January 11, 1982, p. 108.

[2]For a discussion of the survey methodology, see Appendix 2, p. 164.

119

To provide a comprehensive picture of the total effort to boost productivity through human resource programs, we deliberately included more than the so-called Quality-of-Work-Life (QWL) programs.

What distinguishes QWL from other types of human resource programs is the effort to encourage employees to participate in the key decisions that affect day-to-day work patterns. Though the scope of QWL programs is not clearly defined, at its core, QWL recognizes that the person who does the job is the person who knows the job best. QWL programs seek to involve the worker directly in problem solving, in the better design of workflow, in improving production quality. More broadly, the term *QWL* covers not only participation in decision making, but general efforts to stimulate workers by making their jobs more interesting, giving them more control over their own activities, and providing them with a more direct stake in their companies' fortunes.

Although our survey encompasses the range of corporate programs aimed at improving worker performance—from recruitment to work scheduling and organization to compensation—a special effort was made to track worker participation and other facets of the QWL movement. Our survey provides a comprehensive profile of the total corporate effort to boost productivity through human resource programs. It covers the extent of these programs, their essential characteristics, and the number of employees affected. It also covers the reasons why the programs were introduced and how effective they are. Our data also offer the first comprehensive examination of the much discussed QWL movement.

Prevalence of Programs

Our survey results show a movement still in its infancy. Only a minority of corporations have human resource programs to stimulate productivity. And the bulk of activities in these programs is under five years old.[3]

One of our startling findings is how few companies have any formal human resource programs to improve productivity. We estimate that only 14 percent of corporations with 100 or more employees have such programs (that is, only 7,000 out of 49,000 corporations; see Figure 10–1).

Figure 10–1
All Companies with 100 or More Employees

1.4%
Programs in Planning Stage

13.9%
Companies with Programs

84.7%
No Programs

Furthermore, even in companies with programs, 4 of every 10 employees do not participate. Our survey reveals that only one third of all employees in corporations with 100 or more employees are involved in at least one human resource activity such as training, job rotation, and the like. *From our survey, we estimated that only about 13 million workers in companies in the United States are presently included in human resource programs.* The other side of the coin is that 28 million have no such involvement at all (see Figure 10–2).

-----

[3]As defined in our study, the term *program* refers to the full scope of a corporation's efforts to involve its employees. Each program may encompass several activities. For example, a program might include quality circles, formal training sources, job rotation, and an incentive plan.

Figure 10–2
Employment in Companies with 100 or More Employees

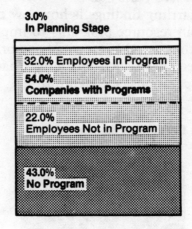

3.0%
In Planning Stage

32.0% Employees in Program
54.0%
Companies with Programs

22.0%
Employees Not in Program

43.0%
No Program

This finding has both pessimistic and optimistic implications. It means that too few people are as yet touched by formal efforts to reach employees and involve them in productivity-raising programs. But it also means that the scope for raising productivity in the future through the implementation of successful human resource activities holds great promise for the American economy.

We found a strong relationship between the size of companies and their adoption of formal human resource programs. NYSE-listed companies, which tend to be the larger ones, had a much higher incidence of programs (indeed four times higher) than the average of all U.S. corporations. But even in NYSE-listed corporations *with* programs, nearly half of the work force is not included.

Prevalence of the programs can be summed up as follows:

- Larger companies are far more likely to have programs than smaller ones (see Figure 10–3).
- Even among companies with programs, only about 60 percent of workers are involved in them.
- For all companies with 100 or more employees, we estimate that only 13 million workers are presently in-

Figure 10–3
Percent of Corporations with Programs (corporations with 100 or more employees)

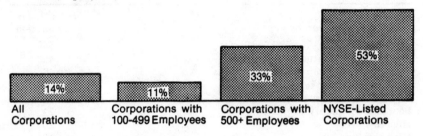

All Corporations	Corporations with 100–499 Employees	Corporations with 500+ Employees	NYSE-Listed Corporations
14%	11%	33%	53%

cluded in some human resource activity and that 28 million have no involvement whatever.

Clearly, we have a long way to go in realizing the full benefits of successful programs across the American economy. That is both a problem and a promise.

Why Programs Were Initiated[4]

Typically, corporations offer several reasons for initiating human resource programs. But, as would be expected, the driving force is the desire to improve competitiveness. Indeed, three fifths of the corporations mentioned cost cutting, and two fifths mentioned productivity improvement—the other side of the cost-cutting coin—as prompting the initiation of their programs. Also no surprise was the importance attributed to poor morale and general complaints about the quality of work life—cited by half the corporations—as factors stimulating interest (see Table 10–1, next page).

---

[4]To maintain statistical reliability, the detailed findings covered in the remainder of this discussion are based on responses of corporations with 500 employees or more. These companies account for 93 percent of the employees covered by programs.

Table 10–1
Why Programs Were Initiated (corporations with 500 or more employees)

Reasons	Percent of All Corporations
Cut costs	58%
Poor employee attitudes/low morale	46
Positive reports from other corporations	40
Productivity improvement	38
Change in management philosophy	36
Poor product quality	24
High turnover	20
High absenteeism	19
Poor service	17
High overtime	12
Lateness	10
Union grievances	8

The most striking response, and perhaps the one of most fundamental significance, is the acknowledgment of a change in management philosophy, especially by the larger corporations. Over one third of all corporations and one half of corporations with 25,000 or more employees reported that the new approach to labor management was initiated because of a shift in management philosophy—that is, a conscious decision to bring about a basic shift in approach to labor-management problems.

By and large, the change in philosophy reflects a shift in existing management's attitude toward human resource programs rather than a turnover in management itself. Only 1 out of every 20 corporations reporting a philosophical change attributed it to an actual change in management. The reported philosophical turnabout is undoubtedly linked to the favorable press received by QWL programs. Two fifths of all respondents and three fifths of the largest corporations gave "positive reports from other companies" as a reason for initiating their own programs.

A potential problem is that the avowed conversion to a new management philosophy may reflect the search for a quick fix for pressing problems rather than a genuine commitment to see a program through to its successful conclusion. One of the survey respondents noted: "Those [programs] will succeed which are tied to [the] basic company style. The gimmicky ones will fail." Another said: "Know your weak areas before you begin any program. Develop an atmosphere where change is accepted and even desired by your employees." Too many efforts are doomed from the start by the failure to adhere to this advice.

Types of Human Resource Activities

Typically, the range of activities encompassed by the human resource programs of large companies is wider than the range for smaller companies—a finding that comes as no surprise. However, the differences in the number of activities moving up the size scale is narrower than one might expect. For example, corporations with over 25,000 employees and those with 5,000 to 25,000 employees both averaged about 10 activities per program. At the lower end of the scale, companies with 500 to 1,000 employees averaged some eight activities, the same as programs of companies with 1,000 to 5,000 employees.[5]

Of the various types of activities covered by human resource programs, the ones most commonly engaged in are the more traditional personnel functions which relate directly to the individual employee's performance. This is underscored in Figure 10–4, which identifies the 15 most common types of activities among all U.S. companies—those both with and without programs.

By far the most widespread human resource activities are formal training and instruction to help telephone skills, the periodic appraisal of the individual employee's performance (practiced by about one quarter of all corporations), and the

---

[5]For a list of typical programs by size and other company characteristics, see Appendix 1, Table A–7, of this book, p. 156.

Figure 10–4
Fifteen Most Common Human Resource Activities (corporations with 500 or more employees)*

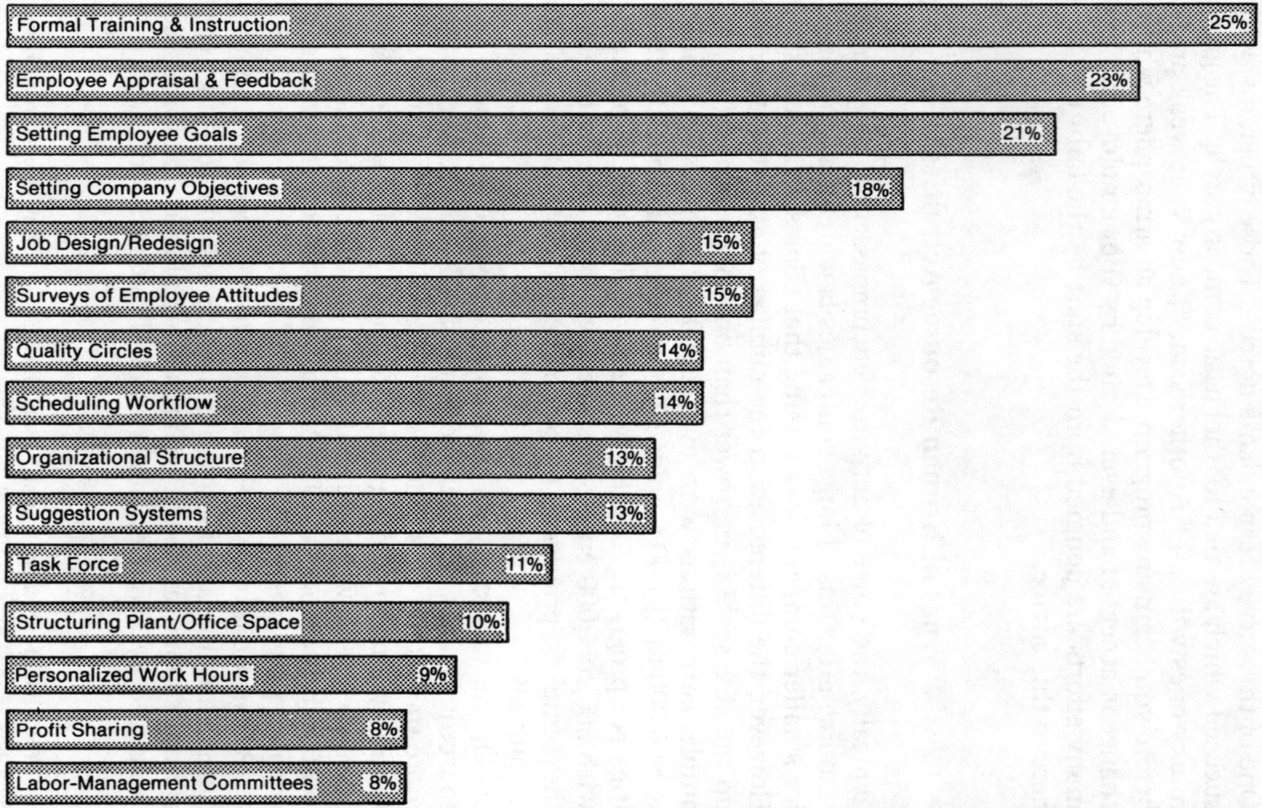

Activity	Percentage
Formal Training & Instruction	25%
Employee Appraisal & Feedback	23%
Setting Employee Goals	21%
Setting Company Objectives	18%
Job Design/Redesign	15%
Surveys of Employee Attitudes	15%
Quality Circles	14%
Scheduling Workflow	14%
Organizational Structure	13%
Suggestion Systems	13%
Task Force	11%
Structuring Plant/Office Space	10%
Personalized Work Hours	9%
Profit Sharing	8%
Labor-Management Committees	8%

*For a complete breakdown of activities by employment size and by manufacturing and nonmanufacturing corporations, see Appendix 1, Table A–8, of this book.

setting of goals for the individual employee (21 percent of all corporations). These activities rank among the top three for all sizes of corporations, although among smaller ones formal training is considerably less widespread than among larger.

In general, differences in participation in any type of activity are strongly related to company size. Those activities that are used far more extensively by large companies (5,000 and more employees) than by small companies include job enlargement, job rotation, production teams, task forces (ad hoc groups set up to tackle specific problems), suggestion systems, quality circles, and employee attitude surveys. For the latter two, disparities between small and large companies are particularly wide.

Another way of dividing these companies is manufacturing versus nonmanufacturing. In this case, the distribution of human resource activities is about the same. Three notable exceptions are quality circles, production teams, and labor-management committees. About 22 percent of all manufacturing firms have quality circles, compared with 8 percent for nonmanufacturing companies; for production teams, the ratios are manufacturing 9 percent, nonmanufacturing 3 percent; and for labor-management committees, they are manufacturing 13 percent, nonmanufacturing, 4 percent.

The QWL Movement

The differences in participation between large and small companies are most pronounced for the newer types of activities associated with the Quality-of-Work-Life (QWL) movement. This is most vividly demonstrated in the case of quality circles—the organization of rank-and-file workers into small groups which meet regularly to analyze, discuss, and solve production-related problems—which have come to epitomize the QWL movement. About 1 in 10 companies in the 500–5,000 employee range have quality circles, compared with 2 of every 10 companies with more than 5,000 employees. Half of all manufacturing companies with 10,000 employees or more have quality circles.

That quality circles and other clearly identifiable QWL activities—particularly job rotation, job enlargement, and production teams—are associated with larger companies reflects the following:

- Smaller companies are more likely to have (or think they have) better informal lines of communication.
- Larger companies with better-developed programs are in a better position to experiment with more novel activities.
- Larger companies are more likely to have concerns about poor employee attitudes, morale, and quality of work life, as reflected in our survey results.

The recent growth in interest in QWL is reflected in the relatively high proportion of QWL-related activities that were initiated within two years of the survey. Most notably, 3 of every 4 companies with quality circles had them for less than two years; and 4 of every 10 for under a year. Table 10–2 presents the six activities which grew most rapidly in that

Table 10–2
Most-Rapidly Growing Human Resource Activities, 1980–82*
(corporations with 500 or more employees)

	Percent of All Corporations Engaged in the Activity			
Activity	*Under One Year*	*One to Under Two Years*	*Under Two Years*	*No Date Given*
Quality circles	45%	29%	74%	10%
Structuring plant, office space	22	28	50	23
Job design/redesign	17	19	36	34
Group incentive plans	13	17	30	14
Task forces	22	10	32	31
Production teams	8	21	29	25

*For a breakdown of activities by age, see Appendix 1, Table A–9, p. 161.

two-year period. All six are activities clearly associated with the QWL movement.

While it is obvious from the data that QWL-related activities are attracting more interest, a count of activities alone cannot measure the extent to which QWL principles are being accepted by industry. To determine that, we asked corporations which of their human resource activities involved non-management employees in decision making—this being the very essence of QWL.

We found that, of corporations with 500 or more employees that have programs, 70 percent engage in at least one activity which involves some rank-and-file workers in decision making. Since one third of corporations with 500 or more employees have programs, then one in four in that size category have at least made a start toward the less-adversarial, more-participative environment associated with QWL.

It must be emphasized that the recent surge in QWL activities has barely tapped the potential benefits that might be derived from a large-scale QWL effort. Even among corporations with relatively heavy QWL involvement, much remains to be done. For example, one manufacturing company that has been a leader in the QWL effort has all of its more than 50,000 employees participating in one or another aspect of its program; but only relatively few workers are covered by the new, more innovative activities such as quality circles (7 percent) and job enlargement (3 percent). Another 60,000-employee company has a program that encompasses the full array of activities, but none reaches more than 2,000 workers, and most reach only several hundred.

Attitudes toward Participative Decision Making

We asked corporations to identify the problems experienced during the early stages of their programs. As expected, the greatest problems were those stemming from employee skepticism and resistance to change at all company levels. Lack of management commitment was encountered by one 10th of the companies and a similar proportion encountered union problems.

Despite these early difficulties, the vast majority of corporations with programs seem to feel that the effort to initiate a QWL program is worthwhile. This is reflected in the response to a question asking for a general assessment of the future of participative management—is it a passing fad or a promising new approach? The response was overwhelmingly favorable (see Table 10–3).

The very positive response of managers who have experience with participative management is encouraging. American business has begun to take the first successful steps toward a new approach to worker participation, worker productivity, and worker morale. However, many impediments—stemming from entrenched practices—remain to a successful worker involvement effort.

Worker involvement programs require a new attitude. They demand a realization that all members of the company must work harmoniously toward common goals. They demand a willingness by management to listen to the advice of people doing the job and to reflect that advice in their decisions. They demand a willingness to abandon a rigidly hierarchical chain of command. They demand a willingness to share power.

Perhaps a new generation of managers, not yet committed to a culture of management by edict, will be more comfortable than their predecessors with a more-open approach to people and a more-consensual, cooperative corporate society.

Table 10–3
Management's Attitude toward Participative Management
(corporations with 500 or more employees)

	Participative Management Is:	
	A Fad Destined to Disappear	*A Promising New Approach*
All corporations with 500 or more employees	3%	82%
Manufacturing corporations	4	83
NYSE-listed corporations	3	77

If so, there is hope that QWL programs will have a long-term payoff in both higher productivity and higher job satisfaction.

Some Advice to Those Considering a Human Resource Program[6]

Productivity improvement requires change. How that change is managed will determine how much improvement occurs, if any. To approach productivity improvement on a quick-fix basis through "a program" seriously limits lasting gains. In reality, productivity improvement needs to be a process, involving all levels and parts of the organization, from top management on down. The process involves education, training, goals, objectives, commitment, measurement, evaluation, and feedback.

It is important to realize that time is not of the essence, except as relates to feedback. This latter exception is important in that individuals need a sense that what is being attempted is worthwhile. Failures and weaknesses need to be recognized and dealt with, but so do successes and strengths. Further, there are many mechanisms which can be applied in the attempt to improve productivity. Each situation in the organization must be viewed as unique, and dealt with accordingly. No one mechanism (project teams, task forces, quality circles, employee publications, suggestion systems, etc.) is universally applicable. More than likely a given situation would benefit from the application of more than one mechanism.

Finally, organizational structure has purpose, as provided for in its design. Circumventing defined responsibility, authority and accountability inherent in the design will inevitably result in a deterioration of performance. To prevent this, productivity improvement efforts must occur as a part of the normal line management structure. Staff support personnel must provide their expertise to that management, with line management making, and being responsible for, decisions.

---

[6]Sheldon L. Beavers, manager of productivity services, Minnesota Power, submitted this response to a survey question asking for advice to companies which might be considering a human resource program. It captures the range of comments offered by the respondents. Additional representative responses are included in Appendix 1, pp. 156–159.

*"Give a new program a chance to succeed. Commit
to the results of the pilot before implementation.
Continue or discontinue based on results."*

a survey respondent

Chapter 11

The Results

To gain a meaningful evaluation of the effectiveness of their
efforts, we asked our respondents to assess the results of their
human resource programs in three ways:

- The impact on productivity of each type of activity.
- The specific types of improvements resulting from the
  overall human resource program.
- A general assessment of whether the programs were successful or not.

Productivity Impact of Individual Activities

The evaluations offered provide strong support for the propo-
sition that a multifaceted human resource program can be
effective in boosting productivity. Because many of the activities are recent, many corporations failed to offer evaluations.
But in most cases, the responses were sufficient to provide a
profile of those activities that show the most promise in
terms of productivity improvement.

Table 11–1 lists those activities with which respondents
have had the best success. It excludes activities which are

Table 11–1
**Ten Activities with the Highest Percentages of "Very Successful"
Ratings for Productivity Improvement (corporations with 500
or more employees)**

	Percent of All Corporations
Personalized hours	44%
Setting company objectives	40
Formal training	37
Task forces	34
Structuring plant and office space	33
Production teams	32
Setting employee goals	32
Scheduling workflow	29
Quality circles	28
Employee appraisal and feedback	28

maintained by fewer than 15 percent of corporations with programs.[1]

The success story of participative management, as shown in Table 11–1, begins with the introduction of some flexibility in setting working hours. That does not mean people drifting in and out whenever they please; it means allowing people to choose their work hours within specified parameters.

Some 40 percent of our survey respondents thought that involving employees in setting company objectives was one of their most successful QWL activities. Next on the "very successful" list came formal training programs. Also rated very highly was employee involvement in task forces to help solve specific company problems in structuring plant and office space and in production teams. The reader will note that there is some overlap here. Production teams are very much like task forces and other employee groups working together to set objectives, to plan space, to set employee goals, and to schedule workflow—all of which appear as separate lines among the activities contributing to productivity improve-

[1]Appendix 1, Table A–10, p. 162, of this book provides the evaluations for the full list of activities covered in our survey.

ment. That is not surprising. The bottom line seems to be an emphasis on all kinds of activities promoting teamwork, on working together—in short, on active employee participation.

What about quality circles? More than 40 percent of the companies that had adopted quality circles offered no evaluation of them. Most of them said candidly that it was too early to pass judgment. But of the remainder, 28 percent rated quality circles as "very successful," and 29 percent thought them "somewhat successful." Only 1 percent of the companies considered quality circles "unsuccessful."

General Improvements Resulting from Programs

To help assess the overall effects of their programs, we asked the respondents to tell us their experience with a dozen people-related factors of managerial concern. Table 11–2 gives the proportion of companies which reported improvement in each of those areas of concern.

Most important, both lowered costs and improved productivity were listed by more than half the corporations. Only

Table 11–2
**Companies Reporting Improvements Resulting from Programs
(corporations with 500 or more employees)**

Area of Concern	Percent of All Corporations
Employee attitudes/morale	67%
Costs	56
Worker productivity	55
Product quality	54
Service	53
Quality of work life	48
Safety	45
Overtime	42
Turnover	39
Absenteeism	39
Lateness	38
Formal grievances	37

one company in seven reported that productivity remained unchanged; of the remainder, about half said it was too early to evaluate the productivity effects and half offered no evaluation.

The highest incidence of improvement in every area of concern except productivity was reported by the smallest companies,[2] precisely the group that is least likely to consider formal human resource programs.[3]

The favorable reports on productivity improvement take on added significance because they are based on reasonably solid data rather than on general impression. Three fourths of the companies reported that they had specific means for measuring productivity; and two thirds of all companies felt they could do so with at least "fair" precision.

Overall Assessment

The corporations were asked to sum up by providing an overall evaluation of their human resource programs (see Table 11–3). More than half of them considered their programs "successful" or "highly successful," and one quarter rated them "partially successful." The number of corporations in the sample reporting "unsuccessful" was so small as to be statistically insignificant.

The Potential

U.S. management is learning fast to adapt worker involvement activities to the American cultural climate. Management is beginning to make a serious effort to obtain the input

---

[2]For productivity, the incidence of improvement did not vary much by size of firm.

[3]Appendix 1, Table A–11, of this book compares reported improvement by company size, p. 163.

Table 11–3
"Overall How Would You Evaluate Your Human Resource Productivity Program to Date?" (corporations with 500 or more employees)

Highly successful	12%
Successful	42
Partially successful	24
Unsuccessful	0
Too early to evaluate	20
No answer	2
	100%

of workers on all types of work-related issues. After all, nobody knows a specific job better than the person who does it. Managers are opening their doors to employees and encouraging more and better teamwork. They are capitalizing on the inherent pride of workmanship. They are providing greater financial incentives to work together toward common goals.

Our survey shows that those who have experience with QWL do not regard it as a fad. But the QWL movement is still in its infancy and the payoff for a QWL effort takes time. Clearly, any widespread benefits of the move toward QWL lie well into the future.

There are some basic and essential ingredients in an effective QWL effort. Employee involvement should not be regarded as just an add-on to an existing program. To be successful, it requires creating a whole new climate of cooperation and involvement from top to bottom. Creating that kind of climate to replace the more autocratic management style of most companies is an enormously difficult challenge.

Obviously, managerial and employee attitudes do not change overnight. Ingrained habits, old hostilities, routinized procedures are not easy to change. Management may hesitate to weaken its authority; labor leaders may perceive a diminution in their influence (though both attitudes appear to be contrary to actual experience). Right now, when American business and labor find themselves pressed by international competitors, is probably a good time to begin to establish a new mutuality of interests.

What is needed, above all, are new lines of communication, a new openness and willingness to share information, and a determination to solve problems together. The most successful programs seem to provide real incentives through some form of gainsharing.

Fortunately, the new QWL and other human resource programs have been largely successful. Our survey results give them good marks for improving productivity and lowering costs. As experience with them mounts, so should their effectiveness. Most companies do not have programs yet, and those that do, tend to have programs limited both in scope of activities and in degree of employee participation.

We estimate that only some 13 million workers employed by corporations with more than 100 employees are presently covered. That leaves 28 million workers in those companies totally unaffected by any type of human resouce activity to enhance their productivity. Since programs are effective in both manufacturing and nonmanufacturing enterprises and for blue-collar as well as white-collar workers, the potential for improving national productivity growth through Quality-of-Work-Life and other human resource programs seems very promising.

The challenge is to convince corporate America that human resource programs are a good investment, which in the long run will benefit not only the individual corporation and its workers but our entire economy. We need to establish a greater sense of common purpose and shared fate in labor-management relations.

Conclusion

The main finding of this book is simply this: There is enormous potential to boost productivity in the workplace by better utilizing people.

In our review of the book's highlights, we will put forward no comprehensive agenda for action. Rather, we want to alert people to some of those areas in which action might be considered.

Gainsharing

Gainsharing, as we have defined it, includes the four main ways of tying all or part of people's incomes to productivity or profits rather than to a fixed wage: individual incentive plans, group incentive plans, profit sharing, and employee ownership. While a company may use aspects of all four approaches, it is important to understand the advantages and disadvantages of each.

Individual Incentives

It should go without saying that there are plenty of situations in which individual incentives are inappropriate—where groups of people directly involved in the work process need to be mutually supportive and where it is impossible to separate the output of one person from that of another. And in fact, companies applying individual incentives are quite aware of this reality. What really distinguishes these companies from those that apply group gainsharing is an orientation toward defining the work group in terms of the smallest human unit directly involved with the work process.

The main advantage of this orientation is that it concentrates the financial incentive where it matters most: on the people whose discretionary effort most determines the level of output. One main disadvantage is that it offers no financial incentives to the indirect workers.

Group Incentives

Group incentives plans have a different orientation. They include all workers in a plant, whether they are directly or indirectly involved in the work process. One danger from this approach is that some workers will resent it if they feel that others are not doing their part. On the other hand, the clear benefit from including all workers in an incentive plan is that everyone will have the motivation to be more productive.

Group gainsharing can be based on measures of physical productivity or on measures of economic productivity. Improshare is an example of a physical productivity plan, while Scanlon and Rucker are examples of economic productivity plans. Physical productivity plans focus workers' efforts on outputs and inputs that are measured in physical units; economic productivity plans use measures of performance based on wages and prices. The advantage of physical productivity plans is that they focus workers' efforts on factors that they can directly influence. The advantage of economic productivity plans is that they are more closely tied to a company's ability to pay.

Profit Sharing and Employee Ownership

Profit sharing and employee ownership are economic productivity plans that are more extreme than Scanlon and Rucker because they tie worker bonuses to a company's bottom line.

Profits can rise even though output per worker-hour may be declining; profits can fall even though output per worker-hour may be rising. For this reason, profit sharing and employee ownership have been criticized as poor motivators of discretionary effort.

Yet these approaches have at least some positive effect on productivity—and they can also serve other company purposes. These include getting special tax benefits in return for capital investment through the medium of ESOPs, providing employees with a supplemental pension plan, getting workers to accept wage concessions under distress conditions, and providing a basis for worker democracy.

Learning from the Japanese

Our discussion of what Americans can learn from the Japanese began with a look at some things that they might learn from us. In particular, we reviewed certain patterns of discrimination in the Japanese workplace that detract from their productivity, most of which would be against the law in this country. Pointing out that the Japanese do a few things wrong is meant primarily as an antidote to the uncritical attitude that prevails among some Americans toward all things Japanese. And even with regard to the many things the Japanese do right, a sense of caution is in order, since theirs is a society that differs in fundamental ways from our own. At most, then, we should adapt but not adopt the Japanese way of doing things.

Schools

One of the things the Japanese do right is schooling their people; the extraordinary effectiveness of their schools is one relatively neglected reason for their high productivity. By comparison, our own schools are failing to provide our young people with the preparation they need to reach their full productive potential. Given the magnitude of the problem, the business community should seriously consider playing a more active role in helping to make our schools more effective.

Training Managers

We found a pattern of training corporate managers in Japan that differs fundamentally from the pattern in the United States. In particular, we found:

- A practice of providing managers-to-be with "front-lines" experience in the basic processes of their company.
- That managers-to-be are required to spend a long apprenticeship in which they acquire not only technical skills but a deeply felt knowledge of the people of their organization.

By contrast, American managers generally serve a much shorter apprenticeship before assuming executive positions and very rarely get anything similar to front-lines experience. As a result, American managers are not so well trained as their Japanese counterparts in the human knowledge of the organizations they run.

The Japanese can make these enormous investments in time and effort in preparing their managers because they know that these people have made a lifetime commitment to the company; accordingly, the Japanese company need have no concern about reaping the full payoff from its investment. American companies have no such advantage. Nonetheless, any American company that wants to rethink its policies in this area might consider the advantages of creating a loyal core of managers who have a marrow-deep knowledge of the organization and how it works. The company might decide that the benefits of this achievement exceed the risks and costs.

Applicability of Japanese Management to the United States

In order to get a better fix on the applicability of Japanese management methods to the American work force, we asked Professor Richard T. Pascale to examine the performance of Japanese-owned companies in the United States. The companies are managed by Japanese nationals but have American work forces. Pascale matched these companies with American run companies that are similar in major respects.

Pascale found that more than in the American firms, Japanese managers showed:

- When reaching a decision, greater interest in the opinions of their employees.
- Greater concern with worker well-being generally.
- Greater concern with product quality.
- Greater effective concern for the job security of their employees.

In effect, the Japanese are simply reminding us of some of the principles of good management.

The NYSE Survey

The New York Stock Exchange (NYSE) has conducted the first broad-based survey of human resource programs to boost productivity, with special emphasis on worker participation and other facets of the Quality-of-Work-Life (QWL) movement. The major survey findings are as follows:

- Only one in seven companies with 100 or more employees has some kind of program.
- The one in seven, however, accounts for just over half of all corporate employees in the United States.
- In companies with programs, typically 60 percent of the employees—some 13 million workers in all—are involved in some facet of the program.

- These 13 million account for fewer than one third of the 41 million people currently employed in corporations with 100 or more employees.
- The larger the company, the more likely it is to have a program.
- The driving force behind human resource programs is to increase competitiveness by improving productivity and cutting costs.
- Many companies report a "change in management philosophy." Their new outlook on labor relations seems linked to favorable reports about the benefits of QWL.
- Quality circles are spreading, particularly among manufacturing firms and large companies. Two thirds of companies with 5,000 or more employees include them in their programs.
- Companies report that their efforts are successful in:
  Increasing productivity.
  Raising morale.
  Reducing costs.
  Improving service.
  Raising product quality.
  Reducing employee turnover, absenteeism, lateness, and grievances.
- Managements consider participative management a significant long-run approach to raising productivity, and not a passing fad.
- Companies typically measure their productivity in a formal way. The largest productivity improvement from QWL was reported by the smaller companies, the group with the lowest incidence of such programs.

The potential for improving national productivity through human resource programs remains large since:

- Most companies have not yet adopted programs.
- Existing programs are limited, and 40 percent of employees that have them are not covered.

- Human resource programs have major effects on productivity growth and improve employee attitudes and morale.

People and Productivity

How can we improve the productivity of our people? Our book points in a few directions, including:

- More effective education of our work force.
- Better training of our managers in the human side of the organizations they run.
- More employee involvement in decision making.
- Sharing the financial gains of better company performance.

The Quality of Life: Both End and Means

This book began by pointing out that there is a vital link between higher productivity and a rise in living standards and that higher living standards are a necessary part of a better quality of life. We can now see from our findings that higher productivity is achieved by improving the quality of life in the workplace itself—when people are better educated, more humanely treated, more involved in decision making, and better rewarded for their efforts.

Thus we find that ends and means are the same: The challenge to corporate America is to improve quality of life in the workplace; by doing so, it will boost productivity—and in that way, help achieve a better quality of life generally.

Appendixes

Appendix 1

The Status of Women in Japanese Society (Chapter 6)

The discussion in the text about the status of women is based primarily on interviews with Dr. Thomas P. Rohlen. Among other scholars, there appears to be little disagreement about the inferior status of women in Japanese society. For instance, in *The Japanese*, Professor Edwin O. Reischauer writes that "the position of women and the relationship between the sexes are aspects of Japanese society that often stir indignation among Western women, particularly Americans." Reischauer adds that "attitudes of male chauvinism are blatantly evident in Japan" and that "there is severe job discrimination against women."[1]

Table A–1 below provides one indication of the comparative status of Japanese and American women. As the table

Table A–1
Comparative Educational Outcomes: Japan and United States *
(in percent)

	Japan[†]		United States[‡]	
	Men	*Women*	*Men*	*Women*
Graduated from high school	90%	91%	73%	77%
Graduated with a B.A. or equivalent	39	12	25	24

* For age group that was 17 in 1974. This table adapted from Thomas P. Rohlen, *Japan's High Schools* (Berkeley: University of California Press, 1983), p. 4.

† Mombushō, *Waga Kuni Kyoiku Suijun* (Tokyo: Okurashō Insatsu Kyoku, 1975).

‡ U.S. Department of Health, Education and Welfare, Education Division, *Digest of Education Statistics* (Washington, D.C.: U.S. Government Printing Office, 1975).

---

[1] Edwin O. Reischauer, *The Japanese* (Cambridge, Mass.: Harvard University Press, 1977), p. 204.

indicates, in the United States about the same percentage of men and women attend high school and college up through the B.A. or equivalent. But in Japan the pattern is very different: a far larger percentage of men (39 percent vs. 12 percent) graduate with a B.A. or equivalent.

The Economics of Japan's Seniority System
(Chapter 6)

The Japanese company pushes out older workers partly because pay scales are based on a seniority system. Given this system, the company will save money if it retires an older worker and replaces him with a lower-paid younger worker. But this means, in effect, that older workers are overpaid in relation to their real productivity. A better solution for all concerned would be to pay the older worker a wage more in line with his productivity. Then the company would find it economical to retain older workers—and society's overall productivity would rise as a result.

IQ and Education in Japan *(Chapter 7)*

In the text, we argue that at least part of the increase in the Japanese IQ is attributable to the improvement in the educational system. This view differs from that of Richard Lynn, author of the article on the Japanese IQ that is referenced in our text. Lynn writes that since "the increase in IQ was present among 6 yr olds . . . it cannot be explained in terms of improvements in education and must be attributed to effects taking place before the age of six."[2] But what Mr. Lynn does

---

[2]Richard Lynn, "IQ in Japan and the United States Shows a Growing Disparity," *Nature*, May 20, 1982, p. 223.

not realize is that improvements in education are precisely one of these effects taking place before age six. At the time the test was given, most six-year-olds had completed two years of schooling which included instruction in reading; whereas in earlier years, most of Japan's six-year-olds did not have the benefit of this schooling.

Math and Science Mean Scores *(Chapter 7)*

The following three tables include all advanced industrial countries whose schoolchildren were given standardized tests in math and science. The results show that:

- Schoolchildren in Japan score highest.
- Their variation ("coefficient of variation") around the mean is among the lowest.
- Their scores are far higher than those of the U.S. schoolchildren.

Table A–2
Math: Thirteen-Year-Olds

Country	Mean Score	Coefficient of Variation
Japan	31.2	.542
Belgium	27.7	.542
Finland	24.1	.411
The Netherlands	23.9	.665
Australia	20.2	.693
England	19.3	.881
Scotland	19.1	.764
France	18.3	.678
United States	16.2	.821
Sweden	15.7	.689

Source: Torstein Husen, ed., *International Study of Achievement in Mathematics: A Comparison of Twelve Countries*, vol. II (New York: John Wiley & Sons, 1967).

Table A–3
Science: Eleven-Year-Olds

Country	Mean Score	Coefficient of Variation
Japan	21.7	.355
Sweden	18.3	.399
Belgium (Flemish)	17.9	.408
United States	17.7	.525
Finland	17.5	.468
Hungary	16.7	.479
Italy	16.5	.521
England	15.7	.541
The Netherlands	15.3	.497
Federal Republic of Germany	14.9	.497
Scotland	14.0	.600
Belgium (French)	13.9	.511

Source: L. C. Comber and John P. Keeves, *Science Education in Nineteen Countries* (New York: John Wiley & Sons, 1973), pp. 159, 108.

Table A–4
Science: Fourteen-Year-Olds

Country	Mean Score	Coefficient of Variation
Japan	31.2	.474
Hungary	29.1	.436
Australia	24.6	.545
New Zealand	24.2	.533
Federal Republic of Germany	23.7	.485
Sweden	21.7	.539
United States	21.6	.537
Scotland	21.4	.664
England	21.3	.662
Belgium (Flemish)	21.2	.434
Finland	20.5	.517
Italy	18.5	.551
The Netherlands	17.8	.562
Belgium (French)	15.4	.571

Source: L. C. Comber and John P. Keeves, *Science Education in Nineteen Countries* (New York: John Wiley & Sons, 1973), pp. 159, 108.

Table A–5
Comparative Patterns of Decision Making in Japanese- and American-Managed Firms *(Chapter 9)*

Boss's Nonroutine- Decisions Method	Japanese- Managed Firms	American- Managed Firms
Decides alone	24%	29%
Gets factual input from subordinates	24	31
Consults with subordinates for opinions and recommendations	52	40

Source: Research by Professor Richard Tanner Pascale.

Table A–6
Comparative Ways of Dealing with Absenteeism in Japanese- and American-Managed Firms *(Chapter 9)*

Absentees Receiving	Japanese- Managed Firms	American- Managed Firms
Fact-finding and counseling	61%	37%
Punishment	16	31
Other	23	32

Source: Research by Professor Richard Tanner Pascale.

Quality Circles Among Japanese-Managed Companies in the United States (Chapter 9)

Very few Japanese-owned firms in the United States have attempted to start quality circles in their U.S. operations. Pascale did not ask firms in 1974–76 about the use of quality circles in the United States; however, JETRO[3] reports that only 20 of the 238 operations they surveyed had implemented quality circles. Additional firms were planning circles in the future—a response, JETRO indicates, to the current widespread interest in circles within the United States. None of

[3]Japan External Trade Organization, "Japanese Manufacturing Operations in the United States," (New York 1981).

the firms revisited by Pascale in 1982 had an established circle program, although one firm will initiate a program once its employees have adapted to the group orientation upon which the circle concept is based.

Pascale's Methodology in Measuring Productivity[4]
(Chapter 9)

Pascale writes:

> Productivity data were collected at each research site. For each industry, managers and outside industry experts were consulted on the fairness and appropriateness of measures to be used. In the manufacturing industries, performance measures were based upon output per unit of labor. (Owing to accounting practices and hidden subsidies provided by Japanese firms to their subsidiaries, financial performance measures, such as costs and profitability, were not utilized in this investigation.) An effort was made to control for extraneous variables such as differences in production technology and economies of scale. In each instance, tasks were chosen which were virtually identical in the Japanese and American companies. For example, in television manufacturing there are important internal design differences between American and Japanese television sets. However, once the TV chassis is assembled, the final assembly process of inserting the chassis into the case and inspecting the set for defects in color, audio, resolution, definition, and so forth, was performed in a virtually identical manner at the two plants. Other extraneous variables, such as the tools used and production line speeds, were also closely comparable at matched sites. As a second example, in the banking industry, teller speed and accuracy rates as a function of each branch's volume of transactions were deemed an appropriate measure of productivity.

---

[4]Richard Tanner Pascale, "Personnel Practices and Employee Attitudes: A Study of Japanese- and American-Managed Firms in the United States." *Human Relations* 31, no. 7 (1978), pp. 610–11.

Table A–7
Typical Programs by Employment Size and Other Company Characteristics* *(Chapter 10)*

500–999 Employees

Formal training and instruction	Job design/redesign
Employee appraisal and feedback	Scheduling work flow
Setting employee goals	Structuring plant, office space
Setting company objectives	Labor advisory groups

1,000–4,999 Employees

Employee appraisal and feedback	Organizational structure
Formal training and instruction	Survey of employee attitudes
Setting employee goals	Bonus
Setting company objectives	Job design/redesign

5,000–24,999 Employees

Formal training and instruction	Setting company objectives
Employee appraisal and feedback	Suggestion system
Setting employee goals	Scheduling workflow
Quality circles	Job design/redesign
Survey of employee attitudes	Organizational structure

25,000 or More Employees

Formal training and instruction	Setting company objectives
Employee appraisal and feedback	Job design/redesign
Survey of employee attitudes	Suggestion system
Setting employee goals	Task forces
Quality circles	Organizational structure

NYSE Listed Corporations

Formal training and instruction	Quality circles
Employee appraisal and feedback	Suggestion system
Setting employee goals	Job design/redesign
Setting company objectives	Organizational structure
Survey of employee attitudes	

All Nonmanufacturing

Formal training and instruction	Scheduling workflow
Employee appraisal and feedback	Suggestion system
Setting employee goals	Job design/redesign
Setting company objectives	Bonus
Survey of employee attitudes	

All Manufacturing

Formal training and instruction	Setting company objectives
Employee appraisal and feedback	Survey of employee attitudes
Setting employee goals	Organizational structure
Quality circles	Scheduling workflow
Job design/redesign	

Table A–7 (concluded)
Typical Programs by Employment Size and Other Company Characteristics* (Chapter 10)

Manufacturers with 10,000 or More Employees

Formal training and instruction	Suggestion system
Quality circles	Setting company objectives
Employee appraisal and feedback	Organizational structure
Setting employee goals	Job design/redesign
Survey of employee attitudes	Task forces

*Typical programs were selected by computing the average number of activities per program and then taking the most prevalent activities in the group. For example, in the 500–999 employee group, programs were comprised of about eight activities—the leading one being formal training and instruction, and the eighth most popular being labor advisory groups.

Some Advice from People Who Have Experience with Programs *(Chapter 10)*

Respondents to our survey were asked for the advice they would give to someone considering an effort aimed at boosting productivity through human resource programs. Here are some representative responses.

> Don't try to move too fast. Be sure mid- and lower-level management is prepared for and can accept change.
>
> Be sure senior management is properly exposed/educated.
>
> Define your objectives and train all levels of management.
>
> Don't give up and get discouraged too easily.
>
> Facilitate design and implementation as opposed to "tops down" mandated approach, i.e. . . . for the most part a user designed and administered process; be patient and recognize it will take time; be prepared to support lower levels beyond what has been done in the past and listen.
>
> Don't rush into it. Take the time to evaluate the multitude of programs available on the market. Choose one(s) that can be personalized and adapted to your company. Devote the time to train your leaders and members. Don't

expect or demand immediate results. Conversion takes time.

Do not rush in too fast. Explore all the options before making a choice. Too many quick fixes on the market.

Be sensitive to the attitudes of employees in the timing of implementation; include top-management role in program presentation; be sure thrust of program is one of positive reinforcement.

They are very worthwhile, but management shouldn't view them as "The" solution.

Do not underestimate the costs or commitment necessary to obtain desired goals.

Obtain top-management commitment. Try many approaches. Learn from successes and mistakes. Don't get hung up on measurement.

Establish an overall corporate commitment and plan—communicate to all employees.

Be honest with yourself about why you are doing program, how will it be supported, and how it can effectively operate in your environment.

Assess organizational climate and build commitment to program by providing accurate information, involve participants in planning and execution of project, and reward them for participation.

Pilot everything. Success in this area involves some risk. Pilot programs can fail without excessive trauma. The removal of the fear of failure breeds success. Pilots facilitate implementation and short-circuit endless planning. (The world is full of good ideas. It has few implementers.)

Don't allow successful programs to atrophy when implementing new or follow-on programs. Success must be sustained in order to provide the foundation for new programs.

Take it one step at a time—build success upon success.

Support of CEO is essential. Must be designed to meet

organization's needs and objectives. Must be understood by employees involved.

Be realistic and have long-term focus—management and systems change are not easily accomplished.

Patience regarding measurement. Visible top-management support. Let them do their own thing.

Push awareness.

Fully explain and discuss any programs with the employees involved; without their full understanding and co-operation, little can be gained.

Careful front work (i.e., planning) management input and then dedicated maintenance, evaluation, and improvement. They should not be entered into casually or with limited support from top management. Pilot programs should be used whenever possible to gauge performance of programs before full commitment is made. Clear outlining of goals and values for those responsible for coordinating and teaching productivity programs.

You have to be willing to accept risk. Must have action-oriented approach.

Analyze problems and potential solutions for *your* company. Design systems to fit your company's needs. Gain top-management and employee support. Make productivity improvement an internal part of management responsibilities, not the responsibility of one person or one committee. Place top priority on good communications.

Plan carefully—no false starts. Training. Outside assistance.

After the program has been identified, planned, and proposed by middle management, have it announced and goal identified by the top executive of the company.

Must believe in what you are doing. Must demonstrate to your employees your commitment to the program through actions. Must have support of lower and middle management. Must ensure proper training and retraining of all employees. Must provide feedback to employees of program.

Utilize the expertise of a proven consultant. Get support of top management. Be willing to invest time and money in training and in the process of participative management.

Plan well and execute on timely basis. Identify company objectives. Analyze current systems in light of objectives. Plan improvement efforts. Implement without fanfare. Evaluate and be prepared to expand pilot program or drop as needed. Avoid quick fixes.

Get some experienced help. If a union business, start with the union. Involve everyone. Assure that productivity measurements are relevant, honest, and tied to bottom-line profitability.

Believe in the worth of the individual employee: their willingness to cooperate, their flexibility, their interest in looking at new assignments. Stress cooperation.

Keep it simple.

Table A–8
Percentage of Corporations Having Specified Activity (Chapter 10)

Activities	Total	Employment Size				NYSE–Listed	Manufacturing		All Non-manufacturing
		500–999	1,000–4,999	5,000–24,999	25,000+		All	10,000+ Employees	
Job design/redesign	15%	17%	13%	15%	18%	21%	9%	31%	12%
Job enlargement	7	7	5	10	11	13	8	20	7
Job rotation	6	5	5	8	13	13	6	24	6
Formal training and instruction	25	25	22	28	29	42	28	60	22
Setting employee goals	21	19	22	24	22	34	22	48	20
Employee appraisal and feedback	23	20	26	27	24	39	25	50	22
Setting company objectives	18	18	18	18	19	30	18	38	18
Structuring plant and office space	10	14	5	11	6	11	13	16	7
Organizational structure	13	12	14	15	14	21	15	34	11
Scheduling workflow	14	15	12	16	13	21	15	27	13
Personalized work hours	9	11	7	7	13	14	9	21	10
Suggestion systems	13	10	12	18	18	25	13	40	13
Labor/management committees	8	10	5	9	13	13	13	25	4
Labor advisory groups	2	3	1	2	3	2	3	4	1
Quality circles	14	12	10	22	21	28	22	52	8
Production teams	5	4	4	10	11	14	9	28	3
Salarying blue-collar workers	2	2	2	4	4	3	3	10	1
Task forces	11	10	10	14	16	21	14	29	9
Surveys of employee attitudes	15	11	14	21	23	29	16	43	14
Financial Incentives									
Piecework	3	3	2	5	5	7	5	14	1
Group productivity	2	3	1	3	6	5	2	8	2
Profit sharing	8	10	6	10	6	12	9	13	8
Stock purchase plans	7	6	7	9	8	17	10	19	5

Table A–9
Age Distribution of Program Activities (Chapter 10)

Activities*	Under 6 Months	6 to under 12 Months	1 to under 2 Years	2 to under 5 Years	5 to under 10 Years	10 Years or More	Don't Know	No Answer
Job design/redesign	5%	12%	19%	20%	6%	4%	4%	30%
Job enlargement	8	5	14	28	7	3	1	34
Job rotation	2	5	6	33	10	10	1	33
Formal training and instruction	3	7	16	29	12	8	2	24
Setting employee goals	3	7	18	31	9	8	4	21
Employee appraisal and feedback	2	6	11	28	15	10	4	23
Setting company objectives	3	6	11	23	18	8	6	26
Structuring plant and office space	8	14	28	11	11	5	1	23
Organizational structure	6	7	12	26	9	4	3	32
Scheduling workflow	3	6	9	33	5	9	6	29
Personalized work hours	3	6	14	38	16	6	1	16
Suggestion systems	9	1	9	16	21	13	2	30
Labor/management committees	4	4	10	22	7	23	9	21
Labor advisory groups		7	8	34	1	25	1	25
Quality circles	15	30	29	11	4	2		10
Production teams	3	5	21	32	6	9	2	23
Salarying blue-collar workers	0	0	3	35	18	13	3	29
Task forces	8	14	10	23	9	4	8	24
Surveys of employee attitudes	6	11	8	20	19	8	2	28
Financial Incentives								
Piecework	0	0	1	8	6	36	22	27
Group productivity	8	5	17	13	3	42	2	11
Profit sharing	2	0	4	6	14	40	2	31
Stock purchase plans	10	2	3	17	26	16	2	45
All activities†	5%	8%	14%	24%	12%	10%	4%	24%

*Numbers may not add to 100 percent because of rounding.
†Weighted average.

Table A–10
How Corporations Rate the Impact on Productivity of Specific Activities (Chapter 11)

Activities*	Percent Distribution				
	Very Successful	Somewhat Successful	Unsuccessful	Too Early to Evaluate	No Response
Job design/redesign	26%	48%	1%	11%	15%
Job enlargement	25	42	1	17	16
Job rotation	24	43	1	9	23
Formal training and instruction	37	40	0	10	13
Setting employee goals	32	40	1	13	15
Employee appraisal and feedback	28	45	1	12	15
Setting company objectives	40	31	0	10	19
Structuring plant and office space	33	32	0	19	16
Organizational structure	26	43	1	10	20
Scheduling workflow	29	37	0	12	21
Personalized work hours	44	32	0	12	12
Suggestion systems	13	49	14	9	16
Labor/management committees	16	55	9	10	11
Labor advisory groups	0	66	0	21	14
Quality circles	28	29	1	36	7
Production teams	32	36	3	10	19
Salarying blue-collar workers	67	15	0	1	17
Task forces	34	35	1	11	18
Surveys of employee attitudes	22	47	3	11	17
Financial Incentives					
Piecework	60	17	3	1	19
Group productivity	18	58	2	16	8
Profit sharing	26	47	5	2	21
Stock purchase plans	14	47	15	12	12

*Numbers may not add to 100 percent because of rounding.

Table A–11
Percentage of Corporations Reporting Improvement in 12 Key Areas of Management Concern (Chapter 11)

| | | Employment Size | | | | | Manufacturing | | |
Areas of Concern	Total	500–999	1,000–4,999	5,000–24,999	25,000+	NYSE–Listed	All	10,000+ Employees	All Non-manufacturing
Employee attitudes/morale	67%	72%	68%	67%	58%	64%	76%	62%	56%
Costs	56	63	52	55	52	54	63	59	47
Worker productivity	55	56	58	54	53	55	56	54	54
Product quality	54	65	44	59	45	46	71	60	34
Service	53	63	46	57	42	47	54	44	51
Quality of work life	48	59	38	49	45	45	54	44	41
Safety	45	57	37	48	30	39	56	40	32
Overtime	42	50	38	42	31	34	41	37	43
Absenteeism	39	54	30	33	36	32	47	35	31
Turnover	39	46	32	39	42	35	45	36	32
Lateness	38	61	22	31	25	24	47	24	28
Formal grievances	37	49	30	33	27	28	45	32	27

Appendix 2

NYSE Survey Methodology

Background

The NYSE survey was conducted among U.S. corporations by the Exchange's Business Research Division during the spring of 1982. The purpose of the survey was threefold: (1) to measure the incidence of human resource productivity programs among U.S. corporations; (2) to estimate the number of employees in those programs as well as the total employed by such companies; and (3) to collect details about the nature of existing programs and the degree of success achieved. The corporate survey frame was constructed from a master list of nearly 65,000 U.S. corporations compiled by Baldwin H. Ward Publications of Petaluma, California. Thomas T. Semon, research consultant in marketing, provided sampling and weighting guidance; Alvin J. Rosenstein, consultant in marketing, moderated focus group sessions. Questionnaire processing and EDP tabulating were the responsibility of Chilton Research Services of Radnor, Pennsylvania. Additional EDP services and word processing assistance were provided by DSI Data Spectrum, Inc. and WANG Laboratories, Inc., respectively.

Preliminary Research

Besides reviewing available printed material, preliminary research for the study consisted of two focus group sessions and a questionnaire pretest. The focus group sessions were held in New York City and Houston. Twenty individuals representing 18 major companies in the forefront of the human resource productivity improvement effort contributed their time to help define the study direction.

Based upon information derived from the focus group sessions, a questionnaire was developed, sent to the focus group participants for review, and pretested with a mailing to 100 randomly selected companies.

Response during pretest was a poor 8 percent. Follow-up telephone calls indicated that most companies without programs had ignored the questionnaire because they assumed it was directed to companies with programs. Some questionnaires were never received by the addressees.

To meet the response problem, the quality of the entire mailing was upgraded, primarily by supplying a mail-back postcard to encourage response from companies without programs and by giving a more personalized appearance to the mailing itself. Only minor changes were required in the wording of the questionnaire. As a result of these changes, the response rate more than tripled to 27 percent.

Corporate and Employee Universes

Before a sample could be selected for the survey, the NYSE Business Research Division first estimated the universe of all U.S. corporations and the total number of employees of this corporate universe.

A primary list of 65,000 U.S. corporations supplied by Baldwin H. Ward was used as the starting point. This list includes only companies which provide financial data to the public. Initially removed were 2,700 corporations for which employee information was lacking or which had fewer than 100 employees. A preliminary sample of 5,778 names was then drawn. In addition, a 100 percent sample of 1,545 corporations comprised exclusively of NYSE-listed companies was prepared. All foreign-based companies, nonbusiness corporations, and duplicates were removed from both samples. Subsidiaries and divisions were joined with parent companies, causing further reductions. Where appropriate, comparable reductions were made among the 62,300 corporations on the primary list as well.

The number of U.S. corporations with 100 or more employees was estimated at 49,000, and the total number of individuals employed by those corporations was estimated to be 41,000,000. These estimates were compared against published U.S. Department of Commerce data and deemed acceptably accurate for study purposes.

Separate estimates were made for the universe of companies with 500 employees or more: 7,020 corporations employing 35,000,000 individuals.

Sample Design

A sampling matrix was constructed by distributing all corporations into a 90-cell matrix based on 10 employee size categories and 9 SIC categories. Because some cells were extremely small, the sampling matrix was reduced to 25 cells. A preliminary sample (already described) of 5,778 names was drawn on an every-nth-name basis within cells. Another sample list of 1,545 NYSE corporations was selected on a 1-in-1 basis.

After reductions (see previous discussion), the two samples were combined to yield a total of 6,131 corporate names, of which 4,372 were separate, unrelated companies (1,429 NYSE-listed) and 1,759 were related subcorporations (subsidiaries or divisions).

Weighted Survey Results

Corporate and employee weights were constructed on a cell-by-cell basis using the general formula:

$$\frac{\text{Total number in cell}}{\text{Number of returns in cell}} = \text{Weight}$$

Because NYSE-listed companies were purposely overrepresented in the sample, they were given reduced weights to restore proportional balance.

In calculating employee weights, companies which would have exerted inordinate influence in their cells because of large numbers of employees, were removed and weighted separately. For the final employee tabulations, the number of employees in each company was multiplied by its employee weight so that each company exerted an influence in direct proportion to its total employees.

The Survey

During March and April of 1982, 6,131 seven-page questionnaires were mailed in several waves. Of this total, 197 or 3.2 percent were returned as undeliverable. The number of separate companies responding to the study was 1,158, a return of 26.5 percent.

Individual cell response rates ranged from 13.8 percent to 42.9 percent. Because of the low number of responses in some cells, a telephone follow-up was conducted to validate the representativeness of the returns. Out of 158 attempted contacts, 100 calls were completed with nonrespondents principally from low-response cells. Overall, 39.0 percent of those telephoned reported having a program of the type being measured, a level so close to the 41.0 percent rate established by the unduplicated respondents that the survey returns were judged to be representative.

While returns from small companies (fewer than 500 employees) were sufficient to estimate their incidence in the corporate universe, these were insufficient to analyze the programs reported. For this reason, responses from the smaller companies were used to estimate the total number of programs but not to analyze program characteristics.

A copy of the questionnaire used for the NYSE survey is available upon request from the Business Research Division, New York Stock Exchange, 11 Wall Street, New York, N.Y. 10005.

Precision of Results

Results of this survey are accurate within certain sampling tolerances. For example, chances are 95 in 100 that the actual proportion of companies with 100 or more employees and a human resource productivity program will not vary from the 13.9 percent estimate by more than 2.1 percentage points (i.e., the proportion could be as high as 16 percent or as low as 11.8 percent). For companies with 500 or more employees, the 32.8 percent incidence estimated is accurate within 4.6 percentage points, and the actual percentage could be as high as 37.4 percent or as low as 28.2 percent. For other data in this survey, sampling tolerances are accurate within 4 to 12 percentage points. Where program activities are compared with one another, differences of 7 to 17 percentage points are needed for a difference to have statistical significance.

Bibliography

Adult Performance Level Project. *Final Report: The Adult Performance Level Study.* Austin: University of Texas, March 1975.

Anderson, Ronald S. *Education in Japan: A Century of Modern Development.* Washington, D.C.: U.S. Government Printing Office, 1975.

Briggs, B. Bruce. "The Dangerous Folly Called Theory Z." *Fortune,* May 17, 1982.

Building a Better Future. New York: New York Stock Exchange, Office of Economic Research, December 1979.

Carlson, Norma W. "Time Rates Tighten Their Grip on Manufacturing Industries." *Monthly Labor Review,* May 1982.

Carnegie Foundation for the Advancement of Teaching. *The Study of The American High School.* Washington, D.C., 1983.

Clark, Rodney. *The Japanese Company.* New Haven, Conn.: Yale University Press, 1979.

Conte, Michael, and Arnold S. Tannenbaum. "Employee-Owned Companies: Is the Difference Measurable?" *Monthly Labor Review.* July 1978.

Cummings, William K. *Education and Equality in Japan.* Princeton, N.J.: Princeton University Press, 1980.

Diekman, Bernard A., and Bert L. Metzger. *Profit Sharing: The Industrial Adrenalin.* Toronto: Institute of Profit Sharing; and Evanston, Ill.: Profit Sharing Research Foundation, 1975.

167

Doyle, Robert J. *Gainsharing and Productivity: A Guide to Planning, Implementation, and Development.* New York: American Management Associations, 1983.

Ellerman, David P. "ESOPS, Second Class Ownership." *Workplace Democracy,* Winter 1983.

"Employee Stock Ownership Plans." Chicago: Arthur Andersen & Co., 1981.

"ESOPS: An Analytical Report." Chicago: Profit Sharing Council of America.

Fein, Mitchell. *IMPROSHARE: An Alternative to Traditional Managing.* Norcross, Ga.: American Institute of Industrial Engineers, 1981.

Fein, Mitchell. "Improved Productivity through Worker Involvement." Hillsdale, N.J.: Mitchell Fein, Inc., 1982.

Forbes, Roy H., and Lynn Grover Gisi. *Information Society: Will Our High School Graduates Be Ready?* Denver, Colo.: Education Commission of the States, March 1982.

Frost, Carl F., John H. Wakeley, and Robert A. Ruh. *The Scanlon Plan for Organization Development: Identity, Participation, and Equity.* East Lansing: Michigan State University Press, 1974.

Gadway, Charles J. *Functional Literacy: Basic Reading Performance.* Washington, D.C.: National Right to Read Effort, 1976.

Gainsharing: A Collection of Papers. Norcross, Ga.: Institute of Industrial Engineers, 1983.

Graham-Moore, Brian E., and Timothy L. Ross. *Productivity Gainsharing: How Employee Incentive Programs Can Improve Business Performance.* Englewood Cliffs, N.J.: Prentice-Hall, 1983.

Harper, F. A. *Why Wages Rise.* Irvington-on-Hudson, N.Y.: The Foundation for Economic Education, 1957

Hatvany, Nina, and Vladimir Pucik. "Japanese Management in America: What Does and Doesn't Work." *National Productivity Review,* Winter 1981–82.

Hewitt Associates, *ESOPS: An Analytical Report.* Chicago: Profit Sharing Council of America.

"How Do We Live with Bigness? Interview." *New Republic,* July 21, 1982.

"How the Japanese Managed in the U.S." *Fortune,* June 15, 1981.

Industrial Engineering Terminology: A Revision, Consolidation, and Redesignation of ANSI Z94 Index and ANSI Z94.1–12. Norcross, Ga.: Institute of Industrial Engineers, Industrial Engineering & Management Press, 1982.

Japan External Trade Organization. "Japanese Manufacturing Operations in the United States." New York, 1981.

Johnson, Richard T. (now Pascale). "Success and Failure of Japanese Subsidiaries in America." *Columbia Journal of World Business,* Spring 1977.

Kelso, Louis O., and Mortimer J. Adler. *The Capitalist Manifesto.* New York: Random House, 1958.

Kelso, Louis O., and Patricia Hetter. *Two-Factor Theory: The Economics of Reality.* New York: Vintage Books, 1967.

"The Labor Givebacks Are Spreading to Steel." *Business Week,* April 12, 1982.

Lesieur, Frederick G. *The Scanlon Plan: A Frontier in Labor-Management Cooperation.* Cambridge, Mass.: MIT Press, 1968.

Lincoln, James F. *Incentive Management.* Cleveland, Ohio: Lincoln Electric Company, 1951.

Lynn, Richard. "IQ in Japan and the United States Shows a Growing Disparity." *Nature,* May 20, 1982.

Maeroff, Gene I. *Don't Blame the Kids: The Trouble with America's Public Schools.* New York: McGraw-Hill, 1982.

Mansell, Jacquie, and Tom Rankin. "Changing Organizations: The Quality of Working Life Process." *Issues in the Quality of Working Life,* September 1983.

Marsh, Thomas R., and Dale E. McAllister. "ESOPs Tables: A Survey of Companies with Employee Stock Ownership Plans." *Journal of Corporation Law,* 1982.

McCrackin, Bobbie, and Sandra Davis. "Employee Stock Ownership Plans: Economic Boon for the Southeast?" *Economic Review,* October 1983.

Metzger, Bert L. *The Future of Profit Sharing.* Evanston, Ill.: Profit Sharing Research Foundation, December, 1979.

Metzger, Bert L. *Increasing Productivity through Profit Sharing.* Evanston, Ill.: Profit Sharing Research Foundation, 1981.

Mitchell, Daniel J. B. "Gain-Sharing: An Anti-inflation Reform." *Challenge,* July/August 1982.

Mitchell, Richard H. *The Korean Minority in Japan.* Berkeley: University of California Press, 1967.

Moore, Brian E., and Timothy L. Ross. *The Scanlon Way to Improved Productivity: A Practical Guide.* New York: John Wiley & Sons, 1978.

Musashi, Miyamoto. *The Book of Five Rings: The Real Art of Japanese Management.* New York: Bantam Books, 1982.

The National Center for Employee Ownership. "Unions and Employee Ownership: A Symposium." Arlington, Va.: January 26, 1982.

Ouchi, William. *Theory Z: How American Business Can Meet the Japanese Challenge.* Reading, Mass.: Addison-Wesley Publishing, 1981.

Pascale, Richard Tanner. "Communication and Decision Making across Cultures: Japanese and American Comparisons." *Admistrative Science Quarterly,* March 1978.

Pascale, Richard Tanner. "Personnel Practices and Employee Attitudes: A Study of Japanese- and American-Managed Firms in the United States." *Human Relations,* 31, no. 7 (1978).

Pascale, Richard Tanner, and Anthony G. Athos. *The Art of Japanese Management: Applications for American Executives.* New York: Simon & Schuster, 1981.

Pascale, Richard Tanner, and Mary Ann Maguire. "Communication, Decision Making and Implementation among Managers in Japanese- and American-Managed Companies in the United States." *Sociology and Social Research*, October 1978.

Pascale, Richard Tanner, and Mary Ann Maguire. "Comparison of Selected Work Factors in Japan and the United States." *Human Relations*, 1980.

Pascale, Richard Tanner, and Mary Ann Maguire. "Japanese Management Practices in the United States." Manuscript prepared for the New York Stock Exchange, 1982.

Productivity and Inflation. New York: New York Stock Exchange, Office of Economic Research, April 1980.

"Productivity Sharing Programs: Can They Contribute to Productivity Improvement?" Washington, D.C.: U.S. General Accounting Office, March 3, 1981.

Rattner, Steven. "A Tale of Two Ford Plants." *New York Times*, October 13, 1981, Section D.

Reaching a Higher Standard of Living. New York: New York Stock Exchange, Office of Economic Research, January 1979.

Reischauer, Edwin O. *The Japanese*. Cambridge, Mass.: Harvard University Press, 1977.

Rohlen, Thomas P. "Japanese Education and Society." Unpublished manuscript, 1982.

Rohlen, Thomas P. *Japan's High Schools*. Berkeley: University of California Press, 1983.

Rohlen, Thomas P. *For Harmony and Strength: Japanese White-Collar Organization in Anthropological Perspective*. Berkeley: University of California Press, 1974.

Rohlen, Thomas P. " 'Permanent Employment' Faces Recession Slow Growth, and an Aging Work Force." *Journal of Japanese Studies*, 1979.

Rohlen, Thomas P. "The *Juku* Phenomenon: An Exploratory Essay." *Journal of Japanese Studies*, 1980.

Rosen, Corey. *Employee Ownership: Issues, Resources and Legislation*. Arlington, Va.: National Center for Employee Ownership, August 1981.

Shareownership 1983. New York: New York Stock Exchange, Office of Business Research, 1984.

Simmons, John, and William Mares. *Working Together.* New York: Alfred A. Knopf, 1983.

"There's More to ESOP than Meets the Eye." *Fortune,* March 1976.

"Unions and Employee Ownership: A Symposium." Arlington, Va.: The National Center for Employee Ownership, January 26, 1982.

U.S. Economic Performance in a Global Perspective. New York: New York Stock Exchange, Office of Economic Research, February 1981.

Volcker, Paul A. Speech presented at the dedication of the John Gray Institute of Lamar University, Beaumont, Texas, November 11, 1983.

Volcker, Paul A. "We Can Survive Prosperity." Speech presented at the Joint Meeting of the American Economic Association-American Finance Association, San Francisco, December 28, 1983.

Weiner, Nan. "The Japanese Wage System." *Compensation Review,* first quarter 1982.

"Will the Slide Kill Quality Circles?" *Business Week,* January 11, 1982.

Wintner, Linda. *Employee Buyouts: An Alternative to Plant Closings.* New York: The Conference Board, 1983.

Yankelovich, Daniel, and John Immerwahr. *Putting the Work Ethic to Work: A Public Agenda Report on Restoring America's Competitive Vitality.* New York: Public Agenda Foundation, 1983.

Index

A

Action teams, 39–40
Adler, Mortimer J., 71
Adopt-a-school programs, 97
Aerocommander, 107
American workers, Japanese opinions on, 111–12
Anderson, Ronald S., 92 n
Apprenticeship, of Japanese managers, 101–3
Art of Japanese Management, 105
Attwood, William, quoted, 99

B

Baldwin H. Ward Publications, 164–65
Beavers, Sheldon A., 131 n
Blue Cross / Blue Shield, home-based employees, 24
Bonuses
  for action teams, 39–40
  calculation under Rucker plan, 55–58
  for employee suggestions, 38–39
  excluded costs under Rucker plan, 51–52
  and increased personnel costs, 52–53
  individual incentives, 19–20
  Lincoln Electric, 62–64
  product quality measure, 40
  quantitative measure of performance, 40
  under Scanlon plan, 45–48
  theme-of-the-quarter plan, 40–41
  under Rucker plan, 49–53
Book of Five Rings (Musashi), 85–86
Briggs, B. Bruce, 86 n

Bullock, Patti F., 8 n, 38 n
Bullock, R. J., 8 n, 38 n
Burke, Edmond, quoted, 91
Businesses; *see* Companies
Buy-back provision, Improshare plan, 31–34

C

Capital equipment, 34–35
Capital investment, stock purchase plans for, 75
Capitalist Manifesto (Kelso and Adler), 71
Carlson, Norma W., 22 n
Chilton Research Services, 164
Chrysler Corporation, employee wage concessions, 77
Clark, Kenneth, quoted, 95–96
College, Japanese attitude toward, 88–90
Comber, L. C., 152 n
Companies
  adopt-a-school programs, 97
  attitude toward participative decision making, 129–31
  changes in management philosophy, 124–25
  curriculum development, 98
  50–50 sharing under Improshare, 30–31
  large versus small, in human resource programs, 127–29
  management of change, 131–32
  new capital equipment, 34–35
  New York Stock Exchange Survey, 164–68; *see also* New York Stock Exchange

Companies—*Cont.*
  potential for human resource programs, 136–38
  prevalence of human resource programs, 120–23
  profit sharing, 59–82
  programs to develop human resources, 119–32
  reasons for starting human resource programs, 123–35
  recruiting from schools, 97
  role in public education, 96–98
  use of gainsharing, 6–8; *see also* Gainsharing
  work-study programs, 97–98
Company sales, and incentive plans, 11
Competition, 71–72
Conte, Michael, 60 n
Core companies, in Japan, 87–88
Corporate and employee universes, 165–66
Corporations; *see* Companies
Cummings, William K., 92 n
Curriculum development, by companies, 98

D

Decision making, participative; *see* Participative decision making
Deere and Company, 11
  individual incentives, 19–21
Deficits, under Scanlon plan, 45–46
Democracy, improved by stock ownership, 79–80
Desoto Southwest, 44–47
Discretionary effort, 4–6
  definition, 5
  failure under gainsharing, 21
Discrimination, harm to productivity by, 88
Don't Blame the Kids (Maerhoff), 96 n
Doyle, Robert J., 8 n, 13, 15–16
Drucker, Peter F., 17
DSI Data Spectrum, Inc., 164

E

East Greenville, Pa., 37
Eastern Airlines, employee wage concessions, 77

Economic Recovery Tax Act of 1981, 73–74
Economic productivity plans
  group incentives, 43–58
  nonprofit-sharing, 47–48
  versus physical productivity, 53–54
  Rucker plan, 48–53
  Scanlon plan, 44–48
Eddy-Rucker-Nickels Company, 48–53
Education
  adopt-a-school programs, 97
  curriculum development by companies, 98
  in Japan, 150–51
  Japanese approach, 141–42
  Japanese company programs, 101–3
  need for effectiveness, 95–96
  primary and secondary in Japan, 91–94
  quality in United States, 94–95
  role of business, 96–98
  work-study programs, 97–98
Education and Equality in Japan (Cummings), 92 n
Education in Japan (Anderson), 92 n
Elitism, in Japan, 93–94
Ellerman, David, 79 n
Emerson, Ralph Waldo, quoted, 25
Employee(s)
  action teams, 39–40
  attitude toward group output, 14
  discretionary effort, 4–5
  distrust of management, 15
  economic productivity plans, 42–58
  effort and reward relationship, 9
  fear of raising standards, 32
  group incentives, 25–58
  guaranteed employment, 65–67
  horizon of financial responsibility, 9, 14
  job-hopping in Japan, 87–88
  job security and gainsharing, 67–69
  Lincoln Electric, 62
  measuring individual output, 23–24
  number in human resource programs, 121–22
  output per worker-hour, 28–30
  participation in management, 129–31

Employee(s)—*Cont.*
  poor performance, 5–6
  rewards for suggestions, 38–39
  shae of business income, 72–73
  stock purchase plan, 64–65
  vesting schedule, 70
  working at home, 24
Employee buyouts
  benefit to democracy, 79–80
  success of, 77–79
Employee Buyouts (Wintner), 78 n
Employee ownership plans, 12, 59–82
  effect on productivity, 140–41
  employee stock ownership, 70–75
  fostering democracy, 79–80
  Liberty Electric, 61–69
  as pension plans, 76
  saving jobs by, 76–79
  stock purchase plans, 75–76
  taming inflation, 81–82
Employee stock ownership plans
  (ESOP), 70–76
  borrowing privileges, 73
  buyout of Hyatt-Clark Industries,
    78–79
  Economic Recovery Tax Act of 1981
    and, 73–74
  tax benefits, 70–75
  Tax Reduction Act of 1975 and, 73
Employee stock ownership trust
  (ESOT), 70
Employee-supervisor ratio, 17
Employment, guaranteed, 65–67
Employment, Japanese discrimination
  in, 86–88
Engels, Friedrich, 71
ESOP, *see* Employee stock ownership
  plans
ESOP Associates of America, 74
ESOT; *see* Employee stock ownership
  trust

F

Falk, Ted, 97 n
Fein, Mitchell, 21 n, 27–31, 35–36, 68
  quoted, 54
Firing for cause, 110
Flexiplace jobs, 24
Ford auto distributors, 107

Ford Company, employee wage concessions, 77
Front-line experience, Japanese managers, 99–100
Full employment policies, 72–73

G

Gainsharing, 3–12
  advantages of individual incentives,
    139–40
  basic forms, 139
  definition, 4
  and discretionary effort, 5, 12
  economic productivity plans, 43–58
  effect on unemployment, 82
  employee ownership plans, 12
  failure of discretionary effort, 21
  group incentive plans, 11, 25–58
  Improshare plan, 26–37
  individual effort, 9–11
  and individual incentive plans, 13–
    17
  and job security, 67–69
  Knoll plan, 36–42
  Lincoln Electric, 61–70
  New York Stock Exchange survey,
    6–8, 60 n, 119–45, 165–68
  number of companies involved, 6–7
  orientation of group incentives, 140
  profit sharing plans, 11–12
  types of, 8–12
Gainsharing (O'Dell), 15 n, 59 n
Gainsharing and Productivity (Doyle),
  8 n, 15 n
General Motors, 78, 99
  employee wage concessions, 77
Graham-Moore, Brian E., 44 n, 47 n
Group incentive plans, 11
  customized plans, 36–42
  economic productivity plans, 43–58
  and individual employees, 14
  physical productivity plans, 25–42
  Lincoln Electric, 65–67
  Scanlon plan, 44–48

H

Harley Davidson, 107

For Harmony and Strength (Rohlen), 101 n

Harper, F. A., 73 n

Hetter, Patricia, 71 n

Higher education, in Japan, 88–90

Highland, Robert, 44 n

Homestead Act, 59

Honda Motors, management work experience, 99–100

Horizon of financial responsibility, 9, 14

Houston, Texas, 165

Houts, Paul, 93 n

Howell, C. Douglas, 77 n

Human resource programs
  experiences with, 156–59
  general improvements, 135–36
  impact on productivity, 133–35
  New York Stock Exchange Survey, 119–45
  potential for, 136–38
  prevalence of, 120–23
  productivity potential, 144–45
  Quality of Work Life movement, 127–31
  reasons for starting, 123–25
  results of surveying, 131–38
  types of activities, 125–27

Husen, Thorstein, 151 n

Hyatt-Clark Industries, 77–79

I

ICA; *see* Industrial Cooperatives Association

Immerwahr, John, 5 n
  quoted, 13

Improshare (Fein), 29 n

Improshare incentive plan, 11, 25–38, 48, 68
  buy-back provision, 31–34
  compared to Knoll plan, 41–42
  50-50 sharing, 31–31
  impact of new capital equipment, 34–35
  measures of labor output, 27
  myths about, 35–36
  output per worker hour, 28–30
  productivity improvement results, 36–37

Improshare incentive plan—*Cont.*
  raising production standards, 31–34

Improved Productivity Through Sharing; *see* Improshare incentive plan

Incentive Management (Lincoln), 61 n

Incentive plans; *see also* Group incentive plans
  company sales and, 11
  gainsharing, 3–12
  individual, 9–10
  profit sharing and employee ownership, 59–82

Individual incentive plans, 13–24
  advantages, 139–40
  bonus plans, 19–20
  examples, 18–21
  future of, 21–24
  and gainsharing, 13–17
  at-home employees, 24
  Maytag Company, 18–19
  measuring employee output, 23–24
  minus factors, 15
  piecework and scientific management, 17–21
  service occupations, 23–24
  validity, 22–23
  Wall Street brokerage firm, 20

Industrial Cooperatives Association, 79–80

Industrial Engineering Terminology, 16 n

Inflation, 80–81

Institute of Industrial Engineers, 16 n

International Study of Achievement in Mathematics (ed., Husen), 151 n

Inventory turns measure, 40

IQ (Intelligence quotient), 150–51

J

Japan
  and American high school graduates compared, 93
  apprenticeship of managers, 101–3
  businesses owned in United States, 105–15
  college education, 88–90
  core company job policies, 87–88
  discrimination
    against women, 86–87

Japan—*Cont.*
  discrimination—*Cont.*
    against youth, 87
    and productivity, 86–88
  education and IQ in, 150–51
  elitism, 93–94
  importance of schooling, 91–94, 141–42
  Korean minority status, 87
  lateral job hopping, 87–88
  lifetime employment, 65–66
  mandatory retirement, 88
  management theory, 92
  management training programs, 99–104, 142
  management work experience, 99–100
  Ministry of Agriculture and Fishery, 100
  productivity, 85–90
  productivity measurement, 154
  roto training experience, 102–3
  and secondary schooling, 92–94
  seniority system, 150
  status of women, 149, and Chapter 6
Japan Airline, 107
Japan External Trade Organization (JETRO), 153–54
Japanese (Reischauer), 92, 149
Japanese companies in America
  concern for quality, 113–14
  consulting with subordinates, 108
  firing for cause, 110
  job rotation, 109–10
  job satisfaction, 111
  job securities, 108–10
  lessons for American firms, 141
  lessons in management, 143
  management decision making, 108–11
  manager-worker relations, 110–11
  quality circles, 153–54
  thoughts on American workers, 111–12
  treatment of women, 111
Japan's High Schools (Rohlen), 92 n, 94 n
JETRO (Japan External Trade Organization), 153–54

Job rotation, 109–10
Job satisfaction, 111
Job saving
  by employee buyout, 77–79
  by wage concessions, 76–77
Job security
  and gainsharing, 67–69
  in Japanese companies, 108–10
Jobs, measuring individual output, 23–24
Johnson, George, 24 n

K

Kawasaki, 107
Keeves, John P., 152 n
Kelso, Louis O., 71–72
Knoll gainsharing plan, 38–42
  action teams, 39–40
  compared to Improshare, 41–42
  employee suggestions, 38–39
  inventory turns measure, 40
  on-time deliveries measure, 40
  plant performance, 40
  product quality measure, 40
  shipments goal measure, 40
  theme-of-the-quarter plan, 40–41
Knoll International, Inc. 37–38
Korean Minority in Japan (Mitchell), 87 n
Koreans, status in Japan, 87

L

Lester, Tom, 44–46
Lincoln, Abraham, 59
Lincoln, James F., 61 n
Lincoln Electric, 12
  basic guidelines to gainsharing, 69
  guaranteed employment, 65–67
  job security and gainsharing, 67–69
  "leopard" policy, 66–67
  personnel policies, 62
  piecerate system, 3–4, 9–11, 16–17, 62–63
  rate of production, 61
  stock purchase plan, 64–65
  supervisor-employee ratio, 17
  yearend bonus, 62–64
  zero-base wage rate, 20–21
Literacy in the United States, 94–95

Lincoln Electric—*Cont.*
Long, Russell, 70, 75–76
Los Angeles, adopt-a-school plan, 97
Lynn, Richard, 93 n, 150–51

M

McCann, Thomas J., 40 n
Maeroff, Gene I., 96 n
Maguire, Mary Ann, 106 n
Management
changes in philosophy, 124–25
employee distrust of, 15
in Japanese companies, 108–11
Japanese educational programs, 101–3
Japanese "Theory Z," 92
Japanese training programs, 99–104, 142
lessons for American firms, 143
training compared to American firms, 103–4
worker participation, 129–31
Manager-worker relations, in Japan, 110–11
Marx, Karl, 71
Mathematics and science test scores, 151–52
Matsushita Electric Company, 100
Maytag Company, 11
individual incentives, 18–19, 20–21
Metzger, Bert L., 9 n, 61 n
quoted, 3
Millbank, Tweed, Hadley and McCloy law firm, 88 n
Mitchell, Daniell J. B., 82 n
Mitchell, Richard H., 87 n
Mitsubishi Aircraft, 107
Musashi, Miyamoto, quoted, 85

N–O

National Assessment of Educational Progress, 94
National Productivity Review, 8
New York City, 165
New York Stock Exchange, 75, 77
Business Research Division, 164–65
corporate and employee universes, 165–66
interviews, 86 n, 89
major survey findings, 143–45

New York Stock Exchange—*Cont.*
precision of survey results, 168
preliminary research, 164–65
scope of survey, 119–20
survey, 6–8, 60 n
survey findings, 119–45
survey methodology, 165–68
survey results, 133–38
survey sample design, 166
weighted survey results, 166–67
New York Times, 105
NYSE; *see* New York Stock Exchange
O'Dell, Carla, 8 n, 13–16, 59–60
One hundred percent bonus, 3–4
On-time deliveries measure, 40
Output per worker hour, 28–30

P

Pan American Airlines, employee wage concessions, 77
Participative decision making, 129–31
success of, 134–35
Pascale, Richard Tanner, 143, 153 n, 154
study of Japanese companies, 105–15
PAYSOP (Payroll stock ownership plan), 73–74
J. C. Penney, 107
Pension plan stock ownership, 76
Performance, poor, 5
Personnel costs, increase in, 52–53
Personnel policies, Lincoln Electric, 62
Physical productivity
versus economic productivity, 53–54
group incentives, 24–42
Improshare, 25–38
Piecerate work system, 3–4, 9–11
Blue Cross/Blue Shield, 24
Lincoln Electric, 62–63
and scientific management, 17–21
Plant performance, 40
Plous, Fitz K., Jr., 24 n
Product quality measure, 40
Production standards
buy-back provisions, 32–34
employee fear of raising, 32
new capital equipment, 34–35
raising, 31–34
Production teams, 134–35

Productivity
advantages of individual incentives, 139–40
of capital and labor, 71–72
drawbacks of discrimination, 88
drawbacks of Japanese college education, 88–90
economic, 43–58
effect of unions, 114–15
group incentives, 25–42
human resource programs, 119–45
individual incentives, 13–24
importance of schooling for, 91–94
improvement through gainsharing, 6–8
improvement under Improshare, 36–37
in Japan, 85–90
Japanese and American compared, 113–14
Knoll gainsharing plan, 38–42
learning from Japanese management, 141
Lincoln Electric, 61
management of change, 131–32
management training policies, 99–104, 142
measuring, 154
output per worker hour, 28–30
potential of human resource programs, 144–45
potential of Quality of Work Life programs, 136–38
production teams, 134–35
profit sharing and employee ownership, 140–41
Productivity Gainsharing (Graham-Moore and Ross), 44 n
Profit sharing, 11–12, 59–82; *see also* Employee ownership plans
disadvantages, 59–60
effect on productivity, 140–41
taming inflation by, 81–82
Profit Sharing Research Foundation, 3, 9 n, 61
Prudential Insurance Company, 97
Putting the Work Ethic to Work (Yankelovich and Immerwahr), 5 n, 13 n

Q

Quality circles
definition, 127
number of companies with, 127–29
success of, 135
Quality of Work Life programs, 124
basics of, 120
characteristics of the movement, 127–29
participative decision making, 129–31
quality circles, 127–28
success of participative decision making, 134–35
success of quality circles, 135
survey findings, 143–45

R

Reagan, Ronald W., 73, 80
quoted, 1, 59
Reischauer, Edwin O., 90 n, 92, 149
Retirement, mandatory, 88
Reuther, Walter, quoted, 81
Rohlen, Thomas P., 87 n, 88 n, 89 n, 90 n, 92 n, 93–94, 99 n, 101–3, 149
Rosenstein, Alvin, J., 164
Ross, Timothy L., 44 n, 47
Roto Japanese training experience, 102–3
Rucker, Allan W., 48
Rucker incentive plan, 11, 25, 27, 45–53
calculating bonuses, 55–58
critique of, 53–54
excluded costs, 51–52
formula, 48–51
value added concept, 49–50

S

Sabo, Richard, 3–4, 61 n
Sargent, G. D., quoted, 43, 53–54
Scanlon, Joseph, 48–49
Scanlon incentive plan, 11, 21, 44–48
deficits, 45–46
ratio of labor costs to sales, 27
Scanlon Way to Improved Productivity (Moore and Ross), 47
Schooling; *see also* Education
business involvement, 96–97

Schooling—*Cont.*
  importance in Japan, 91–94, 141–42
  *Science Education in Nineteen Coun-
    tries,* (Comber and Keeves), 152
Scientific management, 127–21
Scott, Robert C., 48 n, 52–53
Semon, Thomas T., 164
Seniority system, Japanese, 149–50
Service industries, 23–24
Shapiro, Isaac, 88 n, 91 n
Shipments goal, 40
Shirokiya department stores, 107
Sony Corporation, 107, 109
  management education, 102
Stock ownership, 59–82; *see also* Em-
    ployee ownership plans
Stock purchase plan, 75–76
  contrasted with stock ownership,
    70–71
  Lincoln Electric, 64–65
Suggestions, rewards for, 38–39
Supply and demand determination of
    wages, 71

T

Taguchi, Yoshiaki, 89 n, 100 n
Talon, 107
Tannenbaum, Arnold S., 60 n
Tax benefits of employee stock owner-
    ship plans, 70–75
Tax Reduction Act of 1975
Tax Reduction Act Stock Ownership
    Plan (TRASOP), 73–74
Taylor, Frederick W., 17
Testing in mathematics and science,
    151–52
Theme-of-the-quarter plan, 40–41
Toyota auto distributors, 107
TRASOP; *see* Tax Reduction Act Stock
    Ownership Plan
Twain, Mark, quoted, 83

U

Uedagin bank management training,
    102
Unemployment, 82

Unions, effect on productivity and
    quality, 114–15
United Airlines, 107
United States
  business role in education, 96–98
  employees in human resource pro-
    grams, 121–22
  functionally incompetent adults, 95
  Japanese-owned companies, 105–15
  learning from Japanese management
    practices, 141
  management training, 103–4
  number of high school graduates, 93
  quality of schooling, 94–95
  studies of Japanese productivity, 85–
    86
University of Texas, 95

V–Z

Value added concept, 49–50
Vesting schedule, 70
Volcker, Paul, quoted, 81
Wages
  determination in competitive econ-
    omies, 71–72
  employee concessions, 76–77
  and job performance, 56
  steady advance of, 72–73
Wall Street brokerage firm, use of indi-
    vidual incentives, 20
WANG Laboratories, Inc., 164
Ward, Baldwin H., 164
Wheeling Pittsburgh Steel Corporation,
    77
Why Wages Rise (Harper), 73 n
Wintner, Linda, 78 n
Wolverine Worldwide, Inc., 21
Women
  discrimination against in Japan, 86–
    87
  status in Japan, 149
  treatment in Japanese companies,
    111
Work-study programs, 97–98
Workplace democracy, 79
Yankelovich, Daniel, 5–6
  quoted, 13
Yearend bonus, 62–63
YKK, 107, 109, 112

Youth, Japanese discrimination against, 87; *see also* Education *and* Schooling

Zarello, James, 78 n
Zenith Company, 107
Zero-base piecework plan, 4